THE GREY QUILL SOCIETY REVIEW

number three
spring | 2020

The Grey Quill Society Review

Number 3 • Spring 2020

Writings from The Grey Quill Society, the MPTF Writers' Workshop

Published by:
The Motion Picture & Television Fund
23388 Mulholland Drive
Woodland Hills, CA 91364

Cover Illustration by Patricia Santana
Dedication and Whiteboard art by Peter Dunne
MPTF Campus Art by Petar Sardelich

ISBN: 978-0-578-67799-6

www.mptf.com

This Edition of the
Grey Quill Review
is dedicated to
Richard 'Duke' Anderson,
(08/04/25 - 02/03/20)
who, in the Fall of 2012,
petitioned MPTF to develop a
four-week Memoir Writing
workshop for its residents.
With his indomitable charm
and humor, Duke pushed for
four more weeks after that. And,
after that, four more... until
eventually the weekly Grey Quill
Society meetings became
a permanent fixture on MPTF's
Woodland Hills campus.
Well, Duke, it's 2020,
and we're still going strong,
thanks to you.
We hope you are, too,
raising spirits up there
with your puns,
and jamming with the
best jazz cats around.

dunne

Joel Rogosin
1932~2020

your love was ferocious
your joy overflowing
your way of
bringing us
to our knees
with words
never failing

it breaks our hearts
you're gone
tho you've left your smile
you've left your song

ever present grace
ever present soul
ever present
Joel

CONTENTS

Petar Sardelich

FOREWORD

No surprise here, the MPTF Grey Quillers are back at it with their third volume of amazing writing. While the "cast" changes now and then (that's just the way things go in a senior living environment), the Grey Quillers haven't lost their energy and enthusiasm, the writing remains high quality and exciting, and the sense of community and support remains uppermost. I'm always so impressed with their openness to share very personal stories and the trust and respect in each other that is reflected in this attitude. And the stories themselves! If you want to laugh, to cry, or simply to be gobsmacked with wonder, this is the group for you.

Most of the work in *Volume 3* was completed while our spectacular founder/leader Peter Dunne was still on board. He's lately moved on to greener and colder pastures, Golden, Colorado, to pursue two of his passions—his daughter and grandchildren and finishing his own memoir—but left behind a legacy of building and sustaining Grey Quills over eight years, deep friendships, and a tradition of generous listening, being present and connected, open to surprise, and sensitivity to the humanity embedded in the words, thoughts, and feelings being shared with others. We will uphold all of that with our new fearless leader, Victoria Bullock, who is mainly responsible for pulling together this fine volume.

The Grey Quill meeting every Thursday is a space enveloped in trust and compassion, a space where individuals with different backgrounds, different personal stories, and different world views cultivate an atmosphere of openness, tenderness, and empathy. We are caught off guard weekly with the courage and pure bravura of the stories, with readings that frequently leave us gasping for air, and the delight of discovering new things about others, ourselves, and the world. Who could ask for more than that?

—Bob Beitcher
CEO MPTF

My favorite part of the week is Thursday morning. The two hours I spend with the Grey Quill Society at the MPTF campus provides me with enough soul food to last . . . well, 'til about midday Wednesday.

The Grey Quill Society is a memoir-writing class, but it's also so much more. It's a wellness group. It's therapy. It's a creative outlet. It's something we should all be doing—at all ages, all over the world.

Each week the Quills (as we lovingly refer to them) bare their souls. They bravely share their thoughts, feelings, and in some cases, things that have never been shared with anyone else.

We've listened as people write about parts of themselves that they had hidden so deep. Parts they deemed dark, "bad," and essentially unlovable. Memories that dredge up only the worst feelings. The Quills are brave enough to write. It is an act of courage to tell your story. To tell your truth.

They go beyond memoir writing and begin the process of knowing themselves better. Often painful, sometimes funny, but always personal. We cry and laugh and eventually, we heal.

By sharing our stories, we take a very solitary experience and open it up, only to discover how universal it really is.

I first got involved with the group in 2014 after meeting Peter Dunne—the group's creator, leader, and heart and soul—at an MPTF event. He spoke eloquently (which is the only way he ever speaks) about the writing group he had the honor of running at MPTF. I knew, as sure as any rom-com participant does, that I was in love. I needed to witness this group and I told him so. Thankfully he humored me and invited me along.

Jump forward to 2019 and here I am editing the Quill's third *Review* and stepping into Peter's very large shoes (which are Vans). In fact, so large are said shoes that I have decided to merely step next to them. To fill them would be impossible.

Peter Dunne is the indelible ink in our quills. What started as a four-week memoir-writing class back in 2012 turned into this incredible writing group that so many have come to rely on each week. He has been the most special friend and mentor to me. And, I am sure I can speak for all the Quillers when I say that they feel the same.

I realize I have fewer moments and memories to draw on then the rest of the Quillers.

Very often my memoir pieces are centered around "traumatic" high school experiences, but these wonderful women and men never see me as a young woman with so much to learn (which I most definitely do) but rather as an equal.

My life became so much greater, so much more examined, and because of that, so much more understood when I became an honorary member of the Grey Quill Society.

It still amazes me that I have been welcomed with such open arms. They are intelligent, brilliant, creative, and kind people who I learn from every single week. I am honored and moved that they are willing to continue with this group with me at the helm.

The striking, evocative cover comes from Patricia Santana. Inspired by some of the Quill's pieces, she created this incredible piece of artwork. Influenced by the idea that love never really leaves us, I think it sums up this *Review's* theme—*intimacy*—beautifully. In love and in loss we experience intimacy. When we write, we are intimate with ourselves and our readers, and the Quills go beyond being intimate when they share their souls with us.

This *Review* is all encompassing. A little something from and for everyone.

I know as you read, you too will fall in love. The bravery of the Quills never ceases to astound me. Whether they are dealing with love and sex in their 70s—as in Joan Tannen's hilarious piece; recounting incredibly unique childhoods like Ray DeTournay, growing up in a home for pregnant and unwed mothers; or Anne Faulkner's deeply moving and beautiful piece about her sister that she swore she'd never write, but she did, because of the Grey Quill Society.

I hope this book inspires you to write about yourself, your life, successes and failures. I hope you reach out to your family and friends, share your stories and ask them questions. Have those oh so important conversations. Seek to understand and then in turn, to forgive. Yes, others but also yourselves.

But most of all, I hope you love reading it, tell all your friends and the internet, and that people buy millions of copies.

—Victoria Bullock
Editor

PETER DUNNE

THAT BEAUTIFUL THING THAT NEVER DIES

"I want to love again. Be loved again. But it feels wrong, you know? Selfish. No one will ever replace him."

I listen.

"Besides, if I were to love again and then lose again . . . God. And it's stupid. I mean look at me. I'm too old anyway."

We have been down this path before, literally and figuratively. The grounds of the retirement community were designed for walk-talks like ours. It is quiet here, a good and generous quiet, where the groomed landscape wraps its botanical shawl around tired shoulders conferring unrushed contemplation. We weave our way amid the topiary guardians and carpets of color, trusting the languid harmony of familiar surroundings and familiar conversations for intimacy, even understanding.

She is beautiful in every way beauty exists, and I am certain she will never be too old for love or anything else. She seems to be asking for more than love now, and I'm not exactly sure what. Permission maybe? We arrive at the koi pond and choose a small table where water slides over boulders into song, comforting her thoughts. She stares at her hands, graceful and strong, still adorned with a plain gold band. It hurts to see her this way. I wish I could change things.

"How did you get over it?" she asks.

"It?"

"Maggie."

"Oh, first of all it was long ago."

"But you got over her."

"Actually . . ."

"I don't think I could ever do that."

"Actually, I didn't get over her. I never wanted to."

"But, you seem like you have. You seem . . ."

"Happy?"

"Yes."

"Because she's with me all the time."

"But that's the problem, isn't it? I mean I think about Jim all the time."

"Thinking about her wasn't my problem. Trying to stop thinking about her was, until I accepted the reality that I was never going to stop missing her, and that was to be expected."

"So we just have to live with it."

"It's not as horrible as you make it sound. I make Maggie part of my every day life, that's all. She takes walks with me, and she listens to me. She tells me dumb jokes to cheer me up. She gives me confidence, which I always seem to need. She eats and sleeps with me."

"That's living in the past."

"It's living with the past. Preserving us."

"As a ghost."

"No. Ghosts come from darkness . . . anger and fear. Maggie doesn't come to me out of my anger or fear. She comes to me out of my love for her. I made her my Angel."

"Ghosts. Angels. Like being a little girl again with imaginary friends. I need something real. Something alive."

"It's very alive. Love doesn't die. People do. "

She is quiet again, staring at the aquatic ballet beneath the pond's invisible surface. None of this can be comforting for her. What works for me may not for her or anyone else. How can we possibly reassure anyone that peace will come in time? Statistics show that the chances of wives outliving their husbands increase dramatically with every passing year the couple ages. So they know the odds of that happening to them, but knowing the odds can never soften the blow when it does. When they become a statistic and no longer a wife.

"What if someone else comes along? I'm asking for a friend."

"If someone else comes along, make room for that, too. That's not selfish."

"What is it, then?"

"It's desire, and it's normal."

"It doesn't feel normal."

"You think we're too old for that?"

"It's just that . . . no, of course not. Really?"

"Does that embarrass you?"

"I think surprise more than embarrass."

"Why?"

"Look at me. Does this look like desire?"

"The desire I'm talking about has nothing to do with looks. I'm talking about the desire for intimacy."

"You mean sex."

"Not necessarily. We can live without sex, but we cannot live . . ."

"So there's no more sex."

"Let me finish. We can live without sex, but we can't live, really live, without intimacy. At least I can't. It goes beyond exposing my body. I have to be able to expose who I am, deep down inside, and trust the other person to honor that. It's about respect."

"I think Jim was the only person who ever really respected me. Understood me."

"Maggie with me, too. She made me feel okay just being me. And keeping her close now keeps me okay with who I am, still."

"Why is that, you suppose? Why Jim? Why Maggie?"

"You got me. I still wonder how I ever deserved her."

"Maybe we did something right in a previous lifetime."

"Or maybe everyone deserves true love at least once in their life."

She stands, studying the koi swirling like jewels in deep blue honey. She goes into herself. There is sadness in the moment. It is a moment we all have to get used to, over and over, because it comes and goes for a long time.

"What are you thinking?"

"The 'at least once in your life' part. The never again feeling."

"It doesn't have to be. If there's respect again, anything can happen."

"It would be weird, don't you think?"

"To be intimate? No, not weird. Difficult, I think. But necessary, because once we have intimacy, we finally belong."

"To . . . ?"

"To everybody and every thing. To heaven and earth. Belonging, after all, is the ultimate desire, and the ultimate freedom."

The afternoon closes in around us, and we head back. Hues grow more faint, and the evening fragrances beckon our dreams.

"Heaven and earth."

"The best of both worlds."

"Well, I have to admit I never thought about, you know . . . things . . . this way."

"Now you know. Tell your friend."

"Yeah, right." She relaxes and smiles. "I'll tell my friend."

We arrive at a fork in the path leading to the cottages. With a hug, she goes her way, and I mine. Against all earthly logic, I offer what I know I cannot explain.

"You will love again. I promise."

"I hope you're right. But I must say the part about exposing who I am sounds frightening."

"You get good at it."

A moment later she calls over her shoulder.

"I don't know what I would do without you."

"Simple. Make me an angel."

I prepare for bed remembering how I once felt exactly as she feels. The same desperate search for life's meaning. The same confusion and worry. The same emptiness. I don't think there's any way around it. Everyone is the same. Even if everyone is different. My journey may not have been anything like hers. And it probably wasn't as easy as I tell myself. I'm not sure anymore. I try to remember the pleasure more than the pain, I suppose. I only know that time passes and eventually takes the sorrow with it, leaving love behind. And so I pull the covers up with that love, and sleep. For, if it is true that grief is love with nowhere to go, I have created the place for mine to call home. It is right here wrapped around me. Intimately. That beautiful thing that never dies.

JOEL ROGOSIN

SHAPES

The shapes of the night are passing
Flickering
In and out of shadowed corners
Moving slowly and fleeting
Sizes are indistinct
Formlessly looming in silhouette

Short -lived but memorable
Images implanted, lying and stored in memory
They are people of the night
Lined with nuanced textures
They are alone-together
Families, perhaps,
Moving on, with canes, walkers and wheelchairs
Some limping unaided
These are the night people
Briefly shadow puppets

Finding their way along the corridors . . .

THE TRILOGY

Melissa

The marquee goes dark
Grover's Corners is falling asleep again

All flat and folded and hung until the next performance
The characters are caught in freeze-frame

Mr. Webb and Doc Gibbs are enjoying their last cigars of the day
The wives are checking their stoves

The library, the church and the post office are rolled into stacks
of scenery
George and Emily are having their last milkshake at the drugstore
counter

It's all very life-like and nostalgic
As they hold hands briefly before the audience files in

There will be plenty of time for milkshakes and hand-holding
When they meet again at the next performance

Meanwhile, they're rolled up together in faded canvas until
tomorrow's matinee.

Robin

A gold coin spins in the air
Glittering against the night sky
He catches it deftly and shows her the two sides
An Indian chieftain and Lady Liberty
She points across the highway at a small, family-style hotel
He nods, makes a U-turn, finds a place to park
And leans into her for a familiar kiss

Some people drive to Vegas in the night when it's cool
The drinking and gambling are fun
Others for business, buffets and the shows
Then right on cue, here comes the sun

Inside the casino, she's at the slot machines
He's at the craps table nursing free drinks
He waves to her, indicating his wristwatch

Moments later he's asleep in their modest room
A single light burns in the corner
She steps into the room from the bathroom, for a moment is
silhouetted in the doorway

She's wearing an alluring nightgown
She sees him sprawled on the bed, shoeless, and she smiles
She turns off the bathroom light
Then in the darkness she slips out of her gown
And reaches for him
He rolls over and takes her in his arms

The highway finds them in the morning
A few miles, and then a sudden stop
They forgot to leave the key
Never mind—there are mailboxes ahead
And inviting signs advertising low-cost lodging
Where they will sleep another night
As they get into the car, he flips her the gold coin
She drops it between the cushioned seats
They high-five and join the motorcade north
Heading home to Grandma and the kids.

Susan

It's another summer
And they're asleep
In the back bedroom
Naked and entangled
The screen door is ajar
And banging softly
Figs are ripening on the trees
And drying on well-worn cookie sheets
The breeze carries their rich, sweet fragrance
The couple will be stirring soon
But not yet
There's still time for snuggling

UNTITLED

The first scream came early. It was lonesome and abrupt, piercing the dark silence, with more to come night after night. It meant business, that scream. It could have been a man or a woman, which made it even more frightening. And it gave promise of other screams to come, before we were able to sleep again without them.

The variegated screams gave the deafening experience a whole new meaning. Nightly reminders, then echoes, until most of the residents were finished announcing their presence and claiming their space.

The call and response duets gave the term "assisted living" a brand new context.

Soon, they would be poked and prodded with needles, mysterious swabs and whispered instructions: "Turn over please, now turn back; good, very good; on your side, please—do you want the urinal? There's no reason to wet the bed."

Down the hall, three of the men were playing poker, making jokes about "the family jewels" and comparing notes.

They continued to play after the lights were out, unwilling to quit while they were ahead. Muffled noises came from a storage locker nearby as the men put down their opening bets.

They were still playing cards at 3:00 a.m. when the muffled sounds began to fade away. One could swear there was smothered laughter.

But the men were rounded up and sent to their rooms without finding out for sure. They liked to fantasize, "Been there, done that, can't remember." Then it was finally preparation for bed, with embarrassing remnants in the toilets and in the urinals. Sleep came at last, in fragments of memory, where they tossed and turned and greeted each other on busy street corners.

This was a warehouse, each of them soon realized. Every night, the discoveries were made again, in the calling voices of pain, confusion, nostalgia and street talk.

"Fuck you," someone yelled.

"Is that you?" was a reply.

"Is it Monday?"

"It's Wednesday, for Chrissake!"

"What the hell are we doing here? The golf course is heavy with dew, while we kill time making some kind of pathetic lives for ourselves in here."

"Where else would we be? I mean, where else would we be if we weren't here?"

"In that rotten tomb of death and destruction down the street."

And so it went, night after night, where the favorites held fast to what was left of the night crawlers and holdouts.

When they ran out of curses and swear words, they heard and saw things a different way—magnified—until the next night brought them a troubled peace.

PORTSMOUTH

I have never been here before, but I am certain I have been here because I know it so well—the sights and sounds of the historic northeast town . . . family names on storefronts and colorful hand-made window displays . . . zesty smells from the okay-now-but-in-the-winter-Florida hotdog cart on the picturesque square across from the fabled church . . . perhaps I knew it at some other time in some other life or in a dream of tug-boats, ferries, bridges, icy cold slippery streets, gold and orange and yellow fall leaves magically changing, the mom and pop hardware store still delivering cup-hooks, not ready yet for retirement, what would they do . . . ? the cozy harbor, the same seafood restaurant serving fresh comfort food from the same reliable menu for years, the only-for-breakfast place, run by twin spinster sisters waiting to die together when one's time comes, cobblestones and clapboards, shadowed overgrown houses with new upwardly mobile young owners practicing to commute and looking forward, planning to renovate the shadows but preserve the mystery, handsome horses from expensive verdant white-fenced pastures stamping signature hoofprints into coarse-sand beaches, rowboats, catamarans, freight-ers . . . antique everythings, pungent fragrances from the sea and its fish, old-timers impassive and distrusting strangers for no apparent reason, briefly polite locals wearing only jeans and T-shirts dissect-ing scenic tour busloads—"will you look at that bunch with earmuffs and all those woolen layers," developers at war with green, a sushi bar closed, a beer joint called the Officeopen ("Honey, I'm at the office.") broken-down trucks coughing smoke and humbled with dents, can't-be-salvaged motorcycles, worn out and abandoned, weathered splintered wood-paneled station-wagons, dusty vans looking lived-in on vacation or parked off the ground on blocks forever, skies black and blue and sometimes red like bruises, picture postcard sunsets and dawns, everywhere used-brick chimneys and the warm comfort of fireplaces . . . mostly calm, peaceful, quiet - but not so much on week-ends when there's country music . . .

being here could be life-changing for me
if only I could surely be here . . .
or was I here . . .

could I have been . . . ?

if I was here before can I return again
dreaming or remembering . . .
and will I still find it
not forgotten in morning fog
or lost in evening mist
as much as possible preserved
waiting . . .
New England
New Hampshire
Portsmouth.

THANKSGIVING POEM

They're back each asking for a dance
With fragrances, a smile, a glance
They bring some memories from the past
And wistfully hope they will last

Another year, how can that be?
So much to do, so much to see
Remembrances that came and went
Of happy moments saved and spent

There's a face just newly born
There's a smile just barely worn
Learning how to greet each other
How to fit with one another
Some are busy settling in
Others anxious to begin

It won't be long, a year or so
Then everyone will know his place
And there'll be room for all to grow
Within the family tree's embrace

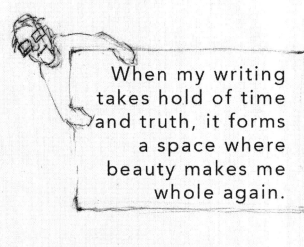

When my writing
takes hold of time
and truth, it forms
a space where
beauty makes me
whole again.

KAY WEISSMAN

A SOLID GOLD RING

A solid gold ring on a chain, nothing more.
They have your shirts, your cufflinks, your wallets, the stuff.
I took your ring on a chain, nothing more.
I remember your deep hazel eyes,
I remember your thunderous laughter,
I remember your caress . . .

A SINGLE TICKET

I bought a single ticket for myself to go see my favorite singer, Audra McDonald. I hadn't gone to see anything by myself since you left me. At first I didn't even remember how to get a ticket. I couldn't find the number for the box office. I just felt frozen, not telling anyone, ashamed that in these two years without you, everything seems harder for me to figure out. You were the one to handle all the little things I hated to do and now I am back to doing it all without your steady, strong hand. I am not who I was then, but I am not sure who I am supposed to be now. I am Kay Weissman, but I am not now known as Mrs. Murray Weissman, and yet I am no longer that young struggling actress excited by every audition, so wanting to please, being knocked down and jumping right back up. You spoiled me by giving me a life filled with love and adventure! I remember thinking that even Princess Diana couldn't be as happy as I was and then, sadly, we all realized that she really wasn't. I was the lucky one, because my happiness lasted until that final awful day we had to say goodbye. I still cannot believe it was really the last goodbye because I feel you beside me all the time. So, as I sat in that single seat, watching an artist we both so admired, I turned to the right of me and then to the left of me to squeeze your hand and share the moment. Although you are no longer physically beside me, you are always with me, so when I venture out once again to see an artist who gives so much pleasure, you will once again be beside me, but I will buy a single ticket. ✒

FIRST DATE

After my first blind date with Murray Weissman I waited three long days until he called me. He invited me to go to a premiere of a movie he was promoting at the Motion Picture Academy. I didn't know what it was to be "promoting" a film and didn't know what to expect. When we arrived at the Academy, he guided me down the red carpet through the shouting paparazzi snapping our pictures. They all seemed to know him and yelled out, "Hey Murray, who's the girl?" I was fifty-nine years old, so just to be called a "girl" was exciting enough, but to walk down a red carpet with paparazzi taking my picture was beyond my wildest imagination. He introduced me to the foreign press as his dear friend and held my hand tightly. He looked at me with love in his eyes. I felt respected, and safe. I was in the right place with the right person. For the first time in my life, I didn't feel I had to do anything except be myself . . . I was enough!

When the movie was over, we skipped the party and went to Kate Mantilini's restaurant down the block. I asked Murray to tell me about himself and he did. He didn't mention anything about his accomplishments or the "business." He talked about his family. His eyes were riveted on mine and they seemed to smile at me. I thought, "This man knows how to love, wouldn't it be wonderful to be loved by him!" It was!!!!!

SEX

When I was around nine years old my mother had "the talk"with me. She told me that when you fell in love with someone, on your wedding day, after the ceremony, when all the guests went home, you and your husband would make love! That was it! I had no idea what she was talking about, and although my mother was a sophisticated woman, she clearly had no idea of how to handle the sex talk.

Love to me was her letting me stay in bed on a Saturday morning and listening to my favorite radio show, *Let's Pretend*. It meant walking hand in hand with my father going to Jeffries Barn in Burbank to watch wrestlers try to kill each other on a Sunday afternoon.

I knew *that* was not what my mother meant, but I also didn't want to hear any details about it either.

I had a group of girlfriends who decided we should tackle this mysterious subject at our next sleepover. The book *Amboy Dukes* by Irving Shulman kept coming up in our research. It was about a gang of tough boys who picked up girls, smoked grass and used dirty language.

Perfect! We heard there were some juicy parts in the book that would explain everything we needed to know. At the sleepover the six of us jumped up on the bed, huddled together, eager to read what would be in store for us on our wedding night. As I recall, Patsy Arnold, the tallest of our group was the chosen reader. I don't remember anything except the part that said, "Her heart started racing as he touched her throbbing breast!"

Patsy stopped reading as we looked at each other and then at the little bumps on our chests. We didn't have a clue, but we blushed and giggled hysterically. Clearly, we were not ready for our tiny breasts to throb, so we ditched the book and got out our stash of *Photoplay* magazines, fantasizing that our lives would imitate the movie stars in the magazines.

Years passed and I became more and more involved in my career. Even if a boy had been interested in me, I would have been oblivious to it. Later, when I danced with Jose Greco, the men in the company were either married or gay, so the subject never came up. When I lived in Spain, my mother was my chaperone so for sure there was no hanky panky going on there.

Back in Miami Beach I began teaching Spanish dancing. I was now in my twenties, very worldly in some ways but still that little naïve girl from Burbank. I became good friends with one of the other dance teachers and, although he and I danced beautifully together, I soon found out that my dear friend was not interested in women. To mend my broken heart, I took a job dancing on a cruise ship heading for Europe. One day, while pining away, I thought I was having a heart attack. I went to see the ship's doctor, Ephthemios Pappayanakos. He didn't speak English and I didn't speak Greek, but by the time we got to the Canary Islands I found out what all the fuss was about!!!! I was now ready for my next adventure!

When I was a little girl, we lived in Miami Beach, close to the area they now call "Little Cuba." It was more like a "Little Ghetto" then, where immigrants—New Yorkers fleeing from the cold and many Jewish socialists flocked to. We lived next door to my *Bubbe* and *Zayde*, Jewish for grandmother and grandfather. My Bubbe used to walk around her apartment saying, *"Oy, hub nicht koyakh,"* meaning "I don't have the energy," when in fact three times a week she walked the mile down Collins Avenue to the beach to do calisthenics which she did with great joy and enthusiasm.

I went with her at age four or five and sat on a nearby bench watching the performance. She never wore a bra and had a loose-fitting bathing suit that hung around her and displayed more than it should have. There were about eight other elderly people in the group. Their esteemed leader was an old man with long white hair. He wore no shirt and had dark leathered skin from too much exposure to the unforgiving Miami sun. He conducted the class like the guru he believed he was. I sat on the bench, my legs dangling, quiet as a mouse as I had been instructed to do, enthralled. They were all immigrants, speaking different languages, smiling and sweating together. My Bubbe fancied herself to be the star of the group, worshipping their magnificent leader who was famous for "only eating fruits and nuts!"

Bubbe was very impressed with herself as well, and her past as a young beauty and actress, but now her passion was collecting money from her neighbors for the National Jewish Fund for Israel. It was a sacred little blue box we called "the *pushke*." This money was to go to Israel, the Promised Land. At every holiday we recited the words, "Next Year in Jerusalem," but no one ever made it there except me, years later.

While my parents worked, my Zayde was my regular babysitter.

I adored him. We also walked down Collins Avenue lined with tall palm trees, but we would then go to a cafeteria. Zayde had his favorite, where he met his cronies every day. I would sit on his lap, my arms wrapped around his ample chest. I loved his smell, a mixture of coffee, cigars, and a little odor of schnapps. I would ask him if I could "walk around on his face." That meant I could take my little fingers and walk around his very wrinkled face as my fingers would sink into his skin. His answer was always yes and the prize would be that he would then kiss each of my little fingers.

When the "boys" came in it was down to business! They spoke in Yiddish but I never minded and sat close to my Zayde, happy as a clam. They would get a glass of hot tea, take a cube of sugar, put it in their mouth and drink the tea. You could then hear "ahhhh" coming from various deep voices. They would then open *The Daily Forward*, a liberal Yiddish newspaper, and begin discussing the news of the day. Heated arguments were filtered with great belly laughs, and although I didn't know a word of what they were saying, I was bewitched at age five.

My Zayde told me many stories, but there was one that I will never forget. He had an older brother, Moishe, who had nine children with his faithful wife, Sarah. It was during the Depression and they were very poor, but every *Shabbos*, Friday night, somehow Sarah would make a fine feast for eleven people using only one chicken. How did she do it? She filled the pot full of carrots, celery, potatoes, rice, and anything else she could find. Everyone got a little piece of chicken in their soup bowl and they were satisfied and happy. One day I asked "Why do you always tell me that story, and how was Aunt Sarah able to do this?"

He said, "I tell you so you will never forget that that's what families do, they take care of each other no matter what."

I said, "What if they can't?"

He answered, "They have to, they are family, when you love someone you fight for them!"

So that's how I grew up, knowing that I would always be taken care of!

I led a gypsy, show business life, full of adventures. At age fifty-nine I met Murray Weissman, the love of my life, and became a member of his family. When he passed away what brought all of us together was no more. My expectations may have been too high! With my Zayde's story still in my heart I was guided to MPTF and found my next family. In the process I found myself again!

"We take care of our own"! My Zayde would be very pleased.

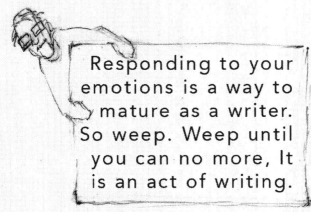

Responding to your emotions is a way to mature as a writer. So weep. Weep until you can no more, It is an act of writing.

LISABETH HUSH

FATTY
(BRANDO)

He'll crawl about
At 4 a.m. turning
Night to day;
Do a phone routine,
Play a little play,
Tapping someone's wires
Greasing up his pole
Courting indiscretion
& secret stores of glow.
Chasing every echo as it
Frogs the throat
Fearless doodlebug
Arranger, out-dined
On shucks & love,
Pissed as an ant taking
Carter's liver pills
Spoiled as a banana peeled
To the slip
Partial to morons
Grease paint blushed
Extra devoted
To polyglot doves,
An eat-n-run rodeo
Neck-'n-neck with time
It's 4 a.m. & I've got
Fatty on my mind.

ACRES

Acres of school girls,
All knowing
Some of their kind got laid,

Watching the parent factories
Prepare the traditional charade

Stories of true love blossom,
Wedding dresses are designed to hide

We've so many primitive rituals
Inculcated into our trip

But the truth of our sexual initiation
Is barred, so we flip.

FIRST TO GO

Think of the widows
Who cry at the grave
"But you promised—
Never to leave me!"

Think of the widows
Who jump in the grave
"It was to be me—
It was to be me!"

I'd like a place
of wood & bone
a geometric home
languishing by the
Mexican Sea
With no single blot
Of color
To halt the mystery

Space

        On

                Space.

TIFFANY

TIFFANY

I TOOK A WALK TO TIFFANY
SUCH AWE I HAD OF TIFFANY.
THE DOORMAN WORE A BADGE, I SAW
"BURNS PROTECTION" GUARDS THIS STORE.
SILVER AND CRYSTAL, GOLD AND BONE
I FINGER - PRINTED EVERYTHING
SMELLED THE POLISHED GLEAMING BRASS,
EDGING THE BEVELED WINDOW MASS/
SANK UPON THE CREWEL COUCH,
WHISPERED THANKS TO ALL THE CRAFTSMEN
AND TO MYSELF WITH NO NEED TO OWN
THE TOYS OF SUBTLY SOCIETY MARKSMEN/
A GIANT GIRL IN PATCHWORK WOOLEN
SMILED AT ME
WATCHING HER SERVICE A DOWAGER LADY
COVETOUS OF A SILVER SWAN FOR GRAVY/

I WALKED AWAY FROM TIFFANY
AND TOOK THE BUS TO WATTS.

(You must be . . . they do not take the bus)

WATTS

THREE SISTERS DIED OF SORROW
THREE MORE WILL TOMORROW
I TOLD 'EM ROSENTHAL IS CHINA,
"BURNS" IS PROTECTION AND
SILVER IS BETTER THAN PLATE,
I SAID , "YOU NEED TRANSFERS, BUT
YOU CAN SPEND THE DAY AS I DO
TRIPPING THE WHITE ANGLO-SAXON WAY
IN THE LAND OF HEAVENLY BILLS.
LOTS OF NOT SO FANCY PEOPLE GET TO PLAY
AT BEING 'MRS. GOLDMINE'
AND DO NOT SPEND A DIME—
SIPPIN' ESPRESSO, PLAYIN' POOL,
WHILE RACKS OF ULTRA CLOTHING
INTIMIDATE THE FOOL
MONEY USES AS ITS TOOL/
THEY CANNOT TELL BY COLOR
THEY CANNOT TELL DRESS,
YOU MUST BE OFFENDED
THEY DO NOT TAKE THE BUS!"

(THAT'S THE SECRET TO SUCCESS)

I FIND A WEALTH OF PLEASURE
STROLLING THRU THAT TOWN,
MEMORIZING LABELS FOR PUTTING
PEOPLE DOWN IN TALK AT SUPPER TABLE/

I KNOW I'M GOING TO DIE
NOT FEELING IS NOT WELL
THE HALLOWED HILLS OF BEVERLY
ARE MY LITTLE TASTE OF HELL.

SOME GUYS REPORT

Some guys report, others stick it
Some gals lay there, others are wicked
Some caps will last, won't give you no bother
A lot of kids call a lot of men father
I got up to write that down
Seems important to have it around
In the morning when I look at life
I'm a hell of a mom, not much of a wife.

I follow the leader, it takes me so long
Dylan quit writing while I'm beginning my song
Blues, lady blues, boots for shoes
Whatever you do, you shouldn't lose
Your desire for international fame
We're all entitled to get the same
Five minutes of prominence MacLuhan says
Each will have before he rests
What year is that? Certainly not last—
My buddy in 'Nam, he got gassed
Now he's famous, guess it's true
Name was Red Foley, he has his due
Holy Foley had to go
Purple Heart, not Romeo
I'd hoped he'd be a better lover
After shooting off his gun
He came back in a box which isn't the same
As getting off his rocks with a particular dame.

Some guys report, others stick it.

It took a second
To rape her
It said in the paper
Even tho her husband
Was home!

"She blew her whistle,

After I shot my, uh, pistol,"
Said the rapist,
"She never even got off
The phone!"

WHALE POEM

S he doesn't cry
For oceans undone

She starts migrating
To bear her a son

Then overcomes sadness
To travel again.

SURE THERE'S STARS

Sure there's stars and I'm indoors
I need a man for company
Some guy who wants to cook and clean my oven
A guy with class who digs my ass
Will wash the dishes and love my cat—

If you think you have the time
We can undo all the pain that's mine
And after that we'll have a try
At fixing you before we die—

Kinda ruff, I know I'm tough
Real cold, ready for that?
When you know you're bad
It makes it easy
To close the door on little guys
Real easy
I'm done with talking, move along
You can watch the stars till dawn.

YOUR JESUS WORSHIP

Your Jesus worship
Is affliction
It aftlicts the
Private you

Your fantasy of
Conversion
Just another
Female Diversion

'The garden will flourish
'The child will grow
But the Husband sours
From tv hours

You left the path
Of nighttime boozing
Gave it up for
Home life oozing

You halo round
The neighborhood
Preaching to the
Sisterhood—

The intimacy you
Seek to sow
Is easily gathered
Because we know
Sharing life has
Frightened you
But you're blue
From talking to
A spook who doesn't
Answer you.

Writing about the darkest times in my life, I can now see that my insecurities were almost always the root of my suffering.

RAYMOND DE TOURNAY

EXCERPT FROM *THE BOY AT BOOTH MEMORIAL*

In 1949, Raymond De Tournay's mother took the position as head nurse at a Salvation Army Home and Hospital where they would live on campus. He was the only boy living among fifty young girls, all pregnant and unmarried. He was fourteen.

There was a note on my dresser. "Rene, Max needs you. Love, Mom."

It wasn't hard to guess the custodian's need as I tracked a trail of pine needles up the stairs to the side door of the hospital. The trail ended in the Great Room where Max was struggling to put a base on the Christmas tree. We tipped it up in place alongside the stained glass window, just where Captain Trudy pointed. It was a big Minnesota Balsam fir with a beautiful shape, just like the trees in the picture books. She sent us down to the suitcase room for the boxes of lights and ornaments. "Jonna wants that too," Max said, pointing to her huge travel trunk.

I wondered what was in Jonna's trunk that could be worth all this effort. I examined the marked out labels, looking for a name or home address but she had done a good job covering her past just like the other girls. I tried the lid to see if it was locked. It was. Jonna had thrown herself fully into the Christmas program and it was clear to see why. After several weeks working in the laundry room she would do anything to get out of that assignment. Even better, this was her line of work.

The Great Room was still a mess. Max had completed the manger and June A. had painted everything. She even did wood grain that made it look like a stable. Several girls had been to the fairgrounds and gotten straw from the cow pens to put on the floor.

Jonna helped me into my Joseph's costume. Mae W., the one about to pop, would play the part of the pregnant Mary. As the choir rehearsed "O Little Town of Bethlehem," Jonna talked us through our moves. Captain Trudy read from her script, speaking softly because of a sore throat. Even though I had no previous experience, I was impressed by how professionally Jonna directed us. She was all business, but I was distracted. For the first time I was close enough to notice the color of her eyes. They were gold.

"Here's where I sing 'O Holy Night,'" Jonna said. "When the light goes off Mae goes off stage, and Veronica takes her place. Mrs. Dardenne puts the baby Jesus in the crib and the choir will sing 'Away in a Manger.'" Veronica L. had just delivered a boy two days ago, which meant she had the freshest baby and the flattest stomach of the residents. As she sat there looking at the empty crib, I wondered if she had made the decision to give him up or not.

"Next we'll sing 'We Three Kings of Orient Are,'" Jonna said. "And girls, I want to remind you not to slouch when you sing. People do notice, so just remember, 'knockers up' at all times." Captain Trudy frowned, but even if she had wanted to say something, she couldn't. "Next, Max comes in and stands next to Joseph," Jonna said.

Max? I couldn't believe it. Jonna had been after him for weeks because he had a real beard. She used her every southern charm but he would not give in.

"I'm Jewish," he said. "I don't belong up there."

Her winning pitch was that Jesus was Jewish, and Max would be an important king from the East carrying rich gifts. He finally agreed but only if he could be a Jewish king. My thought was he's lucky he's not Catholic. I didn't know how I was going to confess this. The penance was going to be huge.

We couldn't complete the rehearsal because Eudora was still working on the narration. It was just as well. Captain Trudy's voice was barely above a whisper. Everyone had a home remedy but she went upstairs to Mom for treatment.

Jonna went over her list. "Max, we need a royal looking headdress for you," she said. "Rene. You look too young. Come early tonight and we'll give you a beard."

Well, that was more like it. I was going to get something out of this. I half wished that Johnny Boy, the bully at school, could see me with a full beard, but knowing him he'd pull my shorts down and show everyone that I was still bald as a baby's ass.

It was already dark and a light snow was falling when I climbed the stairs to the side entrance. The hallway buzzed with activity. Girls ran in and out of the Arts and Crafts room for final fittings of their robes. In the middle was Max, who stood on a table and wore what was once a sheet. The girls had tied it in knots and dyed it with four different colors. When they untied it, the patterns looked exotic, like those in stained glass windows. They called it tie-dye. His costume was the most colorful of all, no doubt. All he needed was a headdress to look like a visiting king.

Jonna was waiting for me. "Put your robe on first, sweet thing," she said. "Now, sit on this stool and don't move." At her elbow was a kitchen bowl filled with hair for my beard. "I need some spirit gum from my trunk," she said to June A.

Right in front of my eyes, she reached in her blouse, searched for a moment in her brassiere and removed a key, just like in my imagination. She handed it to June, who didn't seem to notice that it was burning hot. Jonna leaned down and, with her face close to mine, smeared on spirit gum and began applying the beard. A small bump appeared in my pants.

"Damn," she said, breaking the spell. "We're not going to have enough hair. I might have to put it on your left side only, Rene. Just don't turn toward the audience."

Shirley T. came in with a blanket for the crib. "Did you hear?" she said.

"Margaret's water just broke."

"Oh, just in time," Jonna said. "June, honey. Would you rush upstairs and get me some more material, please. Make sure it's dry."

Max came backstage in his tie-dye outfit. Jonna went to her

trunk, returned with a multi-colored cloth and wrapped it around Max's head like a turban.

"It's a sarong I wore in South Pacific," she said. "I think it's perfect." It certainly was an odd mix of colors and patterns, but I didn't feel qualified to comment. "Besides," she said, "who knows what a Magi looks like anyway."

We could hear people gathering in the anteroom. Major Ellen had invited the director of the Northern Region and other local Salvation Army members, which meant the room would be nearly full. As Jonna's fingers raced across my face, pasting bits of hair over bare skin, Eudora rushed backstage with a bad news look on her face. "Captain Trudy has no voice," she said. "Can't even whisper."

"Oh, shit," Jonna said, emphasizing the T. "It's stage fright. Rene, do you have any ideas?"

I thought for a moment. "How about Colonel Payton?" I said. "He's the guy with the inspection team. I just met him."

"Will he do it?" Jonna asked.

"Probably," I said, with confidence based only on my short time with him. "Have Eudora ask him."

June came back with a bowl of new material. Jonna looked at it and her smile dropped. "We forgot," she said. "Margaret is a redhead."

Jonna's brain went to work. "June, sweetie," she said. "Get the eyebrow pencil and a brush out of my trunk. We can make this work."

As she pasted the new material on my face, June followed right behind with pencil and brush coloring the red hair. When she finished, Jonna looked at my beard critically.

"We've got a pretty good match," she said. "Don't scratch your face and don't let your mother see you. I want her to be surprised."

June looked at my face closely and began to giggle. Jonna gave her a hard look, and she stopped.

Captain Trudy, reduced to hand motions, moved the choir onto risers. Twenty-five girls volunteered to sing. Usually there are only ten so it meant it was a tight fit. They looked beautiful in their white robes, but without question they were all with child. As a final touch, they wore halos that made them look angelic, even if they weren't. Jonna ducked behind stage to change into her robe. In her never-ending effort to be different, she emerged with a sarong over her shoulders, sort of like a shawl. Since she would be standing out front conducting the choir, the extra color would be insurance that no one would miss her.

When the doors opened, the sight of the Christmas tree, the manger, the stained glass window, and the twenty-five-voice choir impressed the audience. Backstage we could hear "oohs and aahs" as they took their seats. Major Ellen made welcoming comments and opened with a prayer. It was a rambling one that thanked everyone but especially God for providing Colonel Payton as a last minute narrator.

I was getting nervous. Not only was I about to take part in a Protestant instead of a Catholic service, but I was also playing Joseph, someone I had only seen as a statue in church. I could imagine Father McGowan's face if he found out. Mae W. waddled backstage and stood on her mark for our entrance. She took one look at me and let out a loud laugh. Several people said "Shh," which shut her up, but I could see her struggling to stifle another laugh. The choir sang "O Little Town of Bethlehem" and Colonel Payton began his narration of the Nativity Story. We walked slowly into the manger scene. Mae sat on a box painted like a wooden bench, and I stood facing her. It was supposed to be a solemn moment but Mae's stomach kept jiggling like a bowl of Jell-O. At first, I thought it was her baby kicking, but then it stopped. When she looked at me, the jiggling started all over again, and it was hard to keep a straight face. Only Captain Trudy's "Ahem," followed by a stern look, kept us under control.

When the music ended, Colonel Payton resumed his narration. The light in the manger went off, Mae W. shuffled out and Veronica L. took her place as post-baby Mary. All we needed was baby Jesus.

Jonna turned to face the audience. Never having heard her sing solo, I was more than curious. She performed "O Holy Night" with the most beautiful soprano voice I had ever heard. Her tone was clear, her expressions and hand gestures clearly said "professional." The audience was visibly moved, Captain Trudy most of all. She sat in the front row using her handkerchief to dab away tears. The applause was loud, long, and well deserved. Jonna, smiling modestly, took two bows before cueing the light for the manger.

On the first notes of "Away in a Manger," I looked down and saw a baby in the crib. I was so fascinated with Jonna's solo that I hadn't noticed Mom sneak in with the infant boy. Veronica stared at this wonderful thing she had done, and tears ran down her cheeks. I wondered if that meant she had already made the decision to give him up. I couldn't tell by the look on her face, but that wouldn't count anyway. It was when that Tuesday arrived, the day she handed her baby over to an expressionless social worker, that we'd know what was really behind that detached look she'd worn all during pregnancy. I was glad I didn't know. It meant I could delay facing my own difficulty with emotional situations. Ever since my experience on the stairs with Joan B., whenever I heard a girl crying I just walked the other way. Was that what I'd do the rest of my life? Fortunately, I didn't have to solve my problem now, but she had only a few days to decide.

The program was going perfectly until Veronica glanced up at me. She looked away quickly but I saw her stomach begin to quiver and shake, just like Mae's, only without the bulge. I riveted my eyes on Captain Trudy, determined not to spoil the moment. I couldn't figure out why these girls behaved so immaturely, especially since they were older than me.

Colonel Payton was doing a great job with the narration despite no rehearsal. With the choir singing behind him, he recited the visit of the Magi. Max entered the manger scene bearing a gift, a sterling soup tureen on a platter. We hoped the audience would imagine it filled with frankincense or myrrh. When Max saw my face, his eyes grew wide, and he started to smile. I cleared my throat and shot him a hard glance, and he got the message.

Colonel Payton began the final narration. Jonna had said she wanted it "tweaked a little" to make the message more contemporary.

Since Eudora had just finished writing it, the "tweaks" hadn't been read or approved by Captain Trudy or Major Ellen, and they both were on the edge of their chairs.

In a solemn voice, Colonel Payton described the dream of the wise men and their decision to return to their own countries without reporting their findings to Herod. "Ancient records show that one of the wise men traveled to the end of the Roman Empire," he said. "He settled in what is now England where he married, raised children and spread the story of the birth of Jesus, especially emphasizing the humble surroundings in which our savior was born. This story passed through their family from generation to generation until it reached William Booth, the founder of our Salvation Army. His ingrained care and concern for the downtrodden, dispossessed, and destitute is what brings us together tonight."

Colonel Payton paused for dramatic effect. "By providing nurture and shelter in their hour of need for these unfortunate young women under our roof, we maintain a direct connection with the events that happened in Bethlehem almost two thousand years ago this very night. It is a connection that must never be broken."

After these emotional words, the choir sang its final carol, "Joy to the World." The audience joined in and sang at full volume through the two encores that it demanded, followed by applause that wouldn't quit.

I saw tears on the faces of Captain Trudy, Major Ellen, and Jonna, each for a different reason. For Captain Trudy, they were tears of accomplishment; for Major Ellen, relief and for Jonna, they were for being back in the spotlight.

For me it was an evening to remember. I'd never been a part of anything so emotional, and it gave me a feeling of family. In addition, it was my first beard, odd reactions and all. I looked for Mom, but she had returned the baby to the nursery. Jonna broke away from the congratulations and handed me a small bottle.

"This is spirit gum remover," she said. "Go home and take that beard off." I complained that I wanted to show it to Mom.

"Go right now," she said firmly. "Get it off before it causes a rash." I enjoyed the attention of walking around in costume dressed as Joseph, but I sure didn't want a rash on my face and left reluctantly. I had just opened the bottle of spirit gum remover when Mom came home. She was excited about the performance and especially my part in it. "I want to see what my boy looks like with a beard," she said. When she came closer, I expected her to break out laughing like the rest. Instead, her eyes got bigger than Max's.

"Get that off your face and do it right now," she said in a very loud voice, emphasizing each word. I didn't think she was worried about a rash. "I'm going back to the hospital," she said. "I want a word with Jonna."

That certainly wasn't the response I had expected, as I'd never seen Mom so mad. I went in the bathroom, looked in the mirror and saw a stranger with a short, curly beard. Reaching up, I ran my fingers through the coarse hair and realized why everyone found it so funny. It was my first close-up look at real pubic hair—only it wasn't mine.

Ray's novel is available through Amazon, Barnes & Noble, Indiebound, North Star Press and, of course, through the author who will autograph each copy with a meaningful sentiment.

THE ROCKY ROAD TO HOLLYWOOD

Just after graduation in June 1956, with my brand new degree in radio and television from Indiana University, I started as a floor-man at the WTTV television studios in Bloomington, Indiana. When I went to the job interview, I was confident, but not cocky. The HR interviewer was properly cool and never tipped his hand except to say that there were five others applying for that position. I was more than pleased when the call came offering the job, and when I asked why I was chosen over the other four candidates, he said, "You have a degree," but he said it like "What in hell did they teach you in college?" So there was my immediate reward for four years of study and depriva-tion. When I asked what the pay was he said, "Minimum wage . . . a dollar an hour." At that rate this job would allow me to continue the deprivation because my salary would be $40.00 a week! After taxes I'd take home $36.35. When I went to the bank I'd throw my check at the teller like it was a dividend on stock investments because I didn't want anyone to know it was my salary.

My first day in professional television was as audio boom operator and all-around gofer on *The Magic Clock*, a daily live children's pro-gram starring a woman and a grandfather clock. She was surrounded and hounded by a cast of characters including an old man, played by a staff announcer and the station artist who dressed in a chicken cos-tume. The booth announcer was the voice of the clock. This was my first exposure to "make it up as you go" unscripted programming as well as the contest of artistic egos. The old man and the chicken were constantly struggling to gain center stage and the bumping contest forced the female star to play the role of a NBA referee.

My contribution was to keep the boom microphone over the action and, since I was degreed, I considered this not a great challenge. I was instructed, during a fade to black, to swing the boom to an adjoining set.

We were in a studio that was a converted truck garage with a very low ceiling. In my desire to show the value of hiring a "certified smart" floorman, I took my cue from the floor monitor and swung the boom smartly to its new position . . . completely ignoring the scoop light that blocked my path.

Even though we were in black, the microphone was hot and made one helluva noise when it hit the scoop and shattered the bulb. What could they do now? It was *live* television! The director faded up on the scene and there was the cast bathed in very dramatic lighting and surrounded by broken glass. Being the pros they were, they immediately made up a story about being in a strange and wondrous land and struggled on to the next commercial. I wish I could remember how they did it but I was too embarrassed to notice.

After the final fade to black, they all had a big laugh at my expense and assured me that these things happen all the time and not to worry about losing my job. Until then I hadn't given that a thought. I was most concerned that they'd deduct the cost of the scoop bulb from my salary and, after my first week as a television professional, I'd end up in the hole.

After striking *The Magic Clock* set, I prepared for the next live event. This was a slam dunk fifteen-minute time filler in the middle of the day called *Coffee Break*. It consisted of a roll-on set with a wall clock, a goldfish in a bowl, and a cardboard sign plugging a local event. Every five minutes or so I'd slide in another sign. Instead of using the big, expensive studio cameras, we were beta testing one of my employer's Vidicon industrial cameras. Vidicon cameras had the ability to stay on a fixed object and never burn in. Unfortunately, if the object had *any* movement, it blurred. The sweep second hand on the clock left a blur. Even the goldfish left a blur but nothing ever burned in. This camera had a heating problem so they left its doors open for ventilation.

That day we had a horrendous summer storm. It caused a power failure and the studio went dark. *Coffee Break* was almost over so I

Raymond De Tournay, seen at left by the camera, was a stage manager at WTTV.

decided to strike the set and the camera and get a jump on the next live setup. I fumbled around for the roll-on set and managed to knock the goldfish bowl off and it broke leaving the poor goldfish flopping in the dark. I then went groping for the camera.

What happened next was an immediate addition to my education—something not provided in college. I didn't know a powerless camera retained an electrical charge, in fact one helluva electrical charge. When my hand went inside the camera's opened door, the stored energy, combined with the wet floor, hurled me through the dark and left me in a crumpled heap against the wall some ten feet away. Just then the lights came on and the crew poured back into the studio and jokingly complained about the new guy taking a nap on company time. I'm not sure I ever told them what really happened. At the end of the day, I'd begun to have second thoughts about my career choice. If my first day was an example of the path to Hollywood, it was going to be one rocky road.

Eventually memoir becomes a search for something more distant than events.

DUKE ANDERSON

A HOLE IN THE WAR

I picked up my mattress and went up the ladders to topside—the flight deck. It was pretty hot in this part of the Pacific at this time of the year and we were in a zone that was now pretty safe from attack. The Japanese had been pushed back from these far western waters for the most part. An occasional submarine might sneak through, but we had a couple of Destroyers (DDs) and a couple of Destroyer Escorts (DEs) as company.

Those DDs and DEs and their sonar would be able to look out for us until we could get to the combat zone and the planes we had picked up in Pearl Harbor would be able to join in the battle. Many of them would go to the bigger carriers who had lost men and planes and were looking for replacements.

I found a place to plunk down my mattress and join some other guys who had the same idea. I tried to get out from below decks as often as I could. Any time I could. To breathe fresh air and see the stars and the moon. The big speakers were playing music from home. As I lay down I could hear The Three Suns and their big hit from home, "Twilight Time."

There were no lights allowed top side, just in case there were enemy subs or planes, only red lights that designated hatches and these couldn't be seen from very far off. Which in a way didn't make much sense, cause if an enemy airplane was above the ship, and if the ship was in waters that had lots of phosphorous, the ship's wake streamed out for miles like a big lighted arrow leading right to the ship's stern.

With no bright lights around, the stars were incredible in their brightness. Around the horizon the stars came down to the waters edge. I could almost read by the light of the stars. We were in pretty calm waters and the rolling of the ship was just another part of life. In fact, when the ship tied up in port it took a while to get used to not having a rolling deck under my feet.

A few of us from the radio shack were in a group and we were talking about home, naturally. Home meant many things. Girls, sports, music, folks, but mostly your girl. After a while I got tired of hearing the same things said over and over. That happens when you are in this small city for months at a time without seeing anyone else from the outside.

I went up to the bow and down a deck to a spot I had discovered that was right under the flight deck, and I could look over and see the ships bow slice through the water. What a beautiful sight, especially when the phosphorous was there. The ship, plowing through that water, created a light that would light up the bottom of the flight deck under which I was standing; light it up enough that I actually could read if I wanted to.

If there were dolphins in the area, they would get covered with phosphorous and as they played around the ship, it was like seeing a bunch of flashlights playing in the water.

I would stand there, my feet spread out a little bit to catch the rolling of the ship and watch the interplay of everything around me. The ship, the stars, the ocean, the dolphins, and me; we all seemed somehow to be connected to each other. It was nice, this peaceful feeling; I could have stayed that way for all my life. So nice. A hole in the war.

COLOR ME PUCE

Emilean was called Lean by her friends and her intimates. Lean was attractive. It was hard to pinpoint her age. When she was rested, she could pass for a young woman.

Lean loved men. And men loved Lean. And Lean loved lean men, mostly. Lean didn't have much luck with her men for some reason. Lean didn't like being alone at all. She hated sleeping alone. She was afraid that some stranger would break into her house and molest her. So, by being married she thought, she would at least know who was molesting her.

Lean was happily married nineteen times. Some of her husbands died at a young age for one reason or another. Some of her husbands bolted during the night, when Lean was asleep, or when she would be standing on the roof of the house, acting the part of a weather vane. They claimed exhaustion, as it turned out Lean wanted to be molested a lot. Not all the time. In her defense it was only during those days of the week that had the letter "a" in them.

Well, Lean got tired of finding, and then losing, husbands. "Enough of that," she muttered to herself. "They're only good for one thing. To take out the trash." So, Lean got herself a dog. That way, she figured, she would have companionship, she wouldn't be alone at night, and her dog could warn her if someone was trying to break into her home. Lean found a great little mutt at the pound. She wanted to name him LB since he came from the pound. But it was hard saying the letters LB. LB came out sounding like ULBGH. So, she named him Herkimer after her ninth husband. Herky became a great friend for Lean. Lean loved sitting on the couch in the evenings, watching her favorite programs, snacking on her favorite, Beef Jerky. Many a pleasant evening was passed in that way. Lean and Herky and Jerking on the couch.

Lean and Herky had become so attached to each other, that Lean would go no place without Herky. She tried that a time or two, but he put up such a fuss that it made them both miserable. It got to the point that she even asked her Therapist-doctor if he would take Herky as a patient. The doctor snorted, "Are you out of your mind?" So, with that snorted retort ringing in her ears, she next asked her Veterinarian if he took people.

Lean hadn't found a restaurant which would allow Herky to eat with her, so often at dinner time, Lean would take Herky in the car and they would go to a drive-through so they could dine together. She would take Herky with her to the Drive-in movies. They were seldom apart. Well, that is until that fateful day when Herky was killed. The tragedy happened at a Chinese restaurant drive-through. While lunging at a wayward egg-roll, Herky accidentally impaled himself on two chopsticks.

Well, Lean was beside herself. Being devastated by her loss, and lonely for a pet, a companion, Lean came up with the idea of getting a chameleon. She had seen people pin them to their lapels. That, she could take with her anyplace.

Oh, maybe some might talk. But she didn't care. So, after shopping around, Lean found a chameleon. They seemed to hit it off right away. She called him Leon. She thought it cute that he could look in two different directions at once, although it made it hard for her to see eye-to-eye with him. However, she reflected, that might come in handy at home. He could keep his eye on her and the door at the same time. She would try to teach him to bark.

Lean and Leon were inseparable. She would take him with her everyplace. Very few people even knew Leon was there. If she wore a green dress, he would change his color to match it. The same with brown, or any other shade. She was able to socialize again. She had missed that. Now, she could go to parties; Leon always there with her. People got used to seeing Lean and Leon together. Leon could keep one eye on Lean, and the other eye could be searching for flies to zap. Sometimes Lean would be doing that too. A different kind of fly. Leon seemed to enjoy seeing Lean wearing different colors. He liked the challenge it gave him. To see if he could match the color, and as a result becoming nearly invisible. Realizing Leon liked the challenge, Lean would wear a color to see if he could correspond. It became a game they played. He always met the contest with success, and then would stare at her with at least one eye as much as to say, "Hah!" Or, whatever word a chameleon would use in that instance. They should have stopped while they were ahead.

What happened was this. Lean dressed and then lovingly and gently placed Leon on her lapel. Leon looked down at her material, and his beady little eyes went crazy. They went this way and that and then his legs straightened out and lifted him up as far away from the cloth as possible and he froze in that position. His mouth lolled open, his eyes got a blank stare and his body shattered into pieces. After they got Lean calmed down, the veterinarian told Lean that trying to merge into the background of the cloth was what had killed Leon. He said, "Lean, you shouldn't have worn plaid."

KILLING

Murder, assassinate, eliminate, terminate, dispatch, finish off, execute. All words we're familiar with. Especially in this day of the mayhem being directed to our homes by television transmitters.

Killing.

I'm against it. Especially if it is directed toward me.

Killing.

We use the word in many ways. A comic will say, "I killed them." A kid will say, "My parents will kill me." A jogger might say, "My feet are killing me." If you get someplace too early you might say to yourself, "I have an hour to kill."

Killing. Being a lifelong and spiritually motivated vegetarian I am against the killing of any animal, fish, or creature. And that would include humans.

Many things can kill. A disease, a heart attack, a war. Especially a war.

There have been many devices invented by man to kill. None more pernicious than a gun.

Guns have killed more people than any other killing instrument. Guns.

The United States Constitution says: A well regulated Militia, being necessary to the security of a free State, the right of the people to keep and bear Arms, shall not be infringed.

The National Rifle Association (NRA) and I disagree on the meaning of this statement. To me a Militia is a body of men, not an individual. To the NRA a militia is any Tom, Dick, or Harry.

The United States has become the most armed nation of individuals in the world. More citizens die from guns than in any other nation. Keep in mind that when the Constitution was written, a gun was a single shot armament. It had to be armed each time it was fired and the arming could take quite a few moments. It's not like the machine guns available now.

What if the Constitution had said instead: A Well regulated Militia, being necessary to the security of a free State, the right of the people to keep and bear a rock, shall not be infringed.

I could live in a nation that has that rule. No guns at all. Just rocks. You couldn't go into a schoolroom and spray a lot of defenseless kids with a rock. You could throw a lot of pebbles, but it wouldn't kill and maim little kids.

Being a fashion conscious people, Rock Stores would be opened. California is often the front runner in new ideas, so Pebble Beach could be the genesis of a chain of Rock Stores. A Rock Store would have all sizes and shapes of rocks. Different colors. Different weights. Small rocks for little kids with small hands. Big rocks for mouth breathers and knuckle draggers.

We could have Rock And Roll coffee shops. You could purchase a rock and have a bagel at the same time.

If putting bodily harm on a person is your intention and you have only a rock you would have to really think about what to do. First of all, you couldn't harm a person from a mile away as you can with a rifle. You would have to be face-to-face with the person. Say it's your brother-in-law. Well, first you couldn't just walk up to him and say, "I'm tired of your stupid face and this rock of mine means business. You've had it, Herkimer; and then hit him." No, it wouldn't always work that way. He might side step. He might run. He might hit you with his rock while you are saying that you are going to hit him. So it could take some planning on your part. You might have to learn how to sidle. Not many can perform a sidle without looking foolish. With enough practice, however, you can sidle with the best. People aren't normally on the look out for a sidler, so the element of surprise can be your friend if you sidle.

As you can see, a rock replacing a gun in society would certainly cut down on the unnecessary deaths we inflict on ourselves each day.

Gangsters, robbers, punk gang members, little tots discovering their parents gun in a drawer, drunks in a bar, wife-beating husbands, husband-beating wives would have a real hard time killing each other with a rock. A bruise here and there, perhaps. But a child wouldn't have lost a parent, a parent wouldn't have lost a child, a family wouldn't have to grieve for a lost member due to a death from a gun.

Why don't we as a nation say—"No more guns." Period. Then we could join hands and sing together our new Anthem—"Rock Of Ages."

I wrote to make the truth bearable and then to make it beautiful and then to make it mine.

ANNE FAULKNER

MY FAILED TEST OF FAITH

I remarried on my thirtieth birthday. I had waited ten years to try again, and got married in church this time. Doug adopted both my boys, so we were all Faulkners. Life was good. Dad hadn't sold the old house I had been raised in, so it was really all good. Doug, me, and the kids moved back to Avalon Drive. Doug still worked at Sears and we both were still involved with the theatre group in town. I got a job at Aeronca Aircraft, the factory Mother had gone to work for when Daddy went into the Army. It was there I had my introduction to computers (but they were nothing like computers today), life was pretty normal for a few months. The boys were going to the same school Bill and I did . . . but without a dog . . . and without walking (those were really the old days).

One day Doug came home and said he was being transferred to Dayton—still doing collections for Sears, but he really didn't want to do that. He wanted to get into sales, and Sears told him they had no openings for sales so he'd have to take the transfer to Dayton or lose the job at Sears. A theatre friend of ours told him to check the TV stations in Dayton 'cause he knew of one that was hiring. Lo and behold, he got that job, and started commuting back and forth . . . probably twenty to thirty miles a day each way—not really sure. When he felt he was pretty settled there, he started looking for an apartment for us. We wanted one that was close to a school for the kids, one preferably that they could walk to each day. I was anxious to quit work in Middletown, and the idea of working for a television station myself really turned me on! It was *like* being an actor and *in* the business . . . at least I'd be as close as I could get—in Ohio! It was November 1963 and we were ready to go! Doug found a wonderful apartment and I loved it. It was two blocks away from school for the kids. Hooray! So we started to move bit by bit, keeping the kids in school where they had started, and trying to stretch our finances. I had quit my job, was managing the house, the packing, the kids. Sometimes I would make a trip up with Doug on the weekend and I'd get Connie to come sleep over and take care of the boys for us. Butch was almost fifteen and they both wanted to take care of themselves but De was only twelve and I did not think they were reliable enough to safely spend the night alone. Connie was eighteen, in her senior year of high school and was as dependable as any adult I knew. She was always available when I needed a sitter. Speaking of Connie . . . she was not a party girl in any way. Even though she was a senior, she never got involved with "after school" anything! She was beginning to talk about college with friends, especially two who were neighbors and in her class. I didn't really know what she was into for fun these last couple years of school.

At any rate, we had both cars loaded to carry the final move of the Faulkners to Dayton. There wasn't room for the boys in the car, so I planned to come back the next morning, after we unloaded the cars, to get them and take Connie back home. The furniture Dad had loaned us was still in the house for any future renter (just as we had used) but I left our little TV so the kids could watch it and called Connie to see if Mom could bring her down. I remember telling her that when we took the last stuff . . . I wanted her to watch the kids because there wouldn't be any room in the car for them going up! But she said no . . . she couldn't come stay with them! She was going out! She said there was a senior party she was going to. I immediately told her that this was important to us, and she had to! I remember she apologized and told me she had baked cookies to take, and Mom was dropping her off. (She didn't drive yet.) I don't remember what I said—I just know that I railed at her. Probably said something like "I'll never forgive you . . ." probably even said "you're not *my* sister anymore" and at any rate hung up on her.

She never called back to apologize and come (which is what I thought she'd do) . . . so I unpacked enough for the boys to get in and we left for Dayton . . . with me so mad, I never called back the whole weekend. I was the adult . . . so put upon. I'm pretty sure it was the first time she'd turned me down, and was the biggest thing I'd asked for.

It was the first bad lesson to learn . . . no excuse . . .

I had no idea that Mother was going to take Connie and her two best friends to Bowling Green, Kentucky, to visit a "teachers" college there. The three wanted to be teachers. So, on Monday morning they had left for their "scope out the college" for next year. Dad was in Argentina . . . or somewhere teaching someone how to make steel . . . ! I didn't care. I was still mad at Connie . . . even thought that if Dad had been there, she would have come! Was wrong again.

At about five that evening, my brother Bill called. He said he had gotten a call and that Mother and Connie had been in an accident. They had driven to Kentucky to check out a couple of schools and coming home, they had had an accident. They were in the hospital in Lexington. He and his wife Libby, were leaving to go there right now, so I should stay put and not worry . . . when they knew something more they would call us! His number had been in Mother's bag . . . so he had been called by the hospital. I simply said, "Doug and I will be there too," and hung up the phone. Friends of ours came and got the boys and we got in the car, and left for Lexington Hospital.

Doug had directions to the hospital. I think I probably smoked a half pack of cigarettes on the way. What on earth happened? Was it really bad? We got to the hospital at about 9:00 p.m. Bill and Libby were in a huge waiting room that we had been directed to. I was surprised how many people were in there, at the time of night. Bill told us that the two girls who had been with Connie and Mother were sitting in the back seat.

Connie was in front, with Mother, and looking back and talking to them. The sun was going down . . . and although Mother could see fine, a farm truck starting to turn to its left had the sun in his eyes and didn't see their car. Mother tried to brake, but too late. The girls in back had seen what was about to happen and just braced themselves against the front seat.

Connie was looking and talking to them, saw nothing and didn't have a seat belt fastened. On impact, the front seat broke and Connie slid off the seat onto the floor and was knocked unconscious, while mother had both knees crash into the dashboard and the steering wheel into her chest. They were both unconscious. That's all the two girls knew. They weren't seriously hurt, but both had broken arms, from bracing themselves I suppose, so they were taken to a local hospital in the area of the crash and Connie and Mother taken to a trauma-equipped hospital in Lexington.

Bill said he had just talked to "one of their doctors." (They each had a doctor.) Mother had a broken rib (or ribs) and was in surgery. So far, that's all he had been told. Then he said "Sis, Connie's doctor said she probably won't live through the night."

"Why?" I said.

Bill said, "She doesn't have any broken bones, but when she fell off the seat, the seat whiplashed her brain, she . . . just . . . isn't . . . going to live."

I insisted on talking to Connie's doctor. I think he said much the same thing Bill told me, with extra words I didn't understand, and ended up saying to me he felt she wouldn't live through the night. I asked if I could see her. He said, "Of course."

He took me into a place . . . I have hard time picturing where it was . . . it wasn't a hospital room . . . at least not a regular hospital room. She was laying on a gurney, I guess. She had a sheet over her . . . up to her shoulders. Obviously, nothing was on her but the sheet. I stood looking at her and held her hand. He said he would be right back, and he left. She looked so normal . . . just asleep. No cuts, no bruises.

I can only remember saying, "I love you, don't you die, Connie" over and over . . . and, "I'm not mad at you Connie. I didn't mean what I said. Please don't die," and then finally, "Wait for me, Connie . . . you *have* to wait for me."

Then I spoke directly to God, "You can't take her. I forbid you to take her."

I'm not really sure how long that went on, I just know I didn't stop ordering *him*. Then I threatened until someone came back into that space we were in.

I wasn't crying, but there were tears, and I went back to the waiting room.

Somehow, I knew what I had to do. *He* wouldn't dare take her away from us, as long as I stayed there to protect her.

It was late by then, and Bill and Doug talked about going to a hotel. I told them I wasn't leaving the hospital. I was calm but determined not to leave Connie. Bill and Libby went to a hotel at about 11:00 p.m. and said they would be back in the morning. Doug stayed with me.

By morning, Connie hadn't died. I had forbade God to take Connie and he didn't. I had won. As long as I stayed at the hospital, it would be okay, Connie would be okay.

I did not leave the hospital for over two weeks, not even to walk outside. I knew as long as I stayed in the hospital, she would get well.

Bill had Armco call my dad and tell him what had happened and fly him home. He got there late Tuesday. Dad encouraged us to go home to our families. I did not share with them why I couldn't leave, I just insisted I was staying, for both of them! Bill and Libby left Wednesday afternoon and so did Doug, to go home to the children. Dad didn't question me, and appreciated I was there with him.

They didn't want Mother to know about Connie while she was still as hurt as she was. They kept her sedated and had me tell her that Connie was okay, she just couldn't get out of bed right now and of course neither could Mother. She had also lost both of her kneecaps —against the dashboard, I guess. The hospital put a cot in Mother's room, a private room, and that's where I slept at night. Dad went to a hotel every night but was with Mother and I every day.

After a week, Dad went back to Middletown and Armco as everyone was in an uproar. John F. Kennedy had been shot and killed that first Friday of their accident. Not even that terrible day had much effect on me.

Every day, mother would ask me if I'd seen Connie and I'd make things up. She never questioned my excuses why Connie couldn't be brought to see her. I knew I had saved Connie's life and she was going to wake up soon.

The story with the doctors hadn't changed. Connie had a brain injury, was still unconscious, and because of the severity, might never wake up. Her brain showed absolutely no activity, but she was still alive and of course, "There is so much we don't know about the brain, you never know." Dad went home through the week and came back on the weekends. I felt surely it wouldn't be long before we could all go home.

When the doctors proposed telling Mother the truth, I was the only one there. Her doctor had kept her partially sedated, but it was still very hard. The doctor said she probably wasn't aware of what she said, but I knew better. She had looked right at me and said, "It should have been you." I turned away. The doctor later said she was so sedated she probably didn't know what she was saying.

She knew. It was her truth. It was never spoken about again and stayed just between us for the rest of her life.

Finally, after another week, Dad and Doug came back. Dad had made arrangements to take Connie and Mother by ambulance to a hospital in Middletown, and Doug finally took me home.

I didn't realize then that bad decisions might have consequences.

At first Dad took Connie and Mother to the hospital in Middletown and I went home to Dayton, my new home. Dad had Mother at home eventually and Bill and his family were there with them for support. I never told any member of my family what I had done regarding my demands to Connie, and to *God*. I hadn't even left the hospital for one minute, even to go out for dinner with Dad.

Consequences that did happen, that lasted for another ten years for her and everyone who loved her, and an additional twenty years for me. What happened later, was the long story of an adjusted new life for everyone and their differences, in consequences.

Dear Connie:

At eighteen, you are on the threshold of a vast experience. In a way,
these past years, have prepared you
for this future. Going back, I remember that as a child you were excep-
tionally sweet ... as I'm sure every
family feels about their own. You
seemed to possess a little too much
tenderness, and a little too much
shyness, but those were traits that
seemed to meld with your personality.
As you grew older, you cried at movies as well as at touching television
dramas ... pitied ... no, protected
almost vehemently those handicapped
or less fortunate than yourself. The
teenage dances were fun, though you
sometimes felt a wallflower and any
wild rides or late hours associated
with the teenage image, didn't appeal
to you at all.
I laughed at your indecision for
your future. You loved visiting the
rest homes for the aged but were
crushed when the final sleep came
to the very sick ... or old. You
were torn between becoming a social

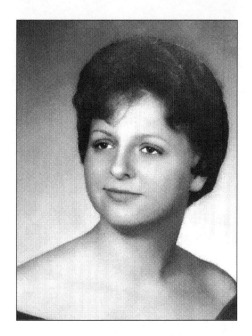

Connie

worker, or a teacher. I wondered, when
you decided to become a third-grade
teacher, whether or not you were influenced by the fact that you were held
back a year...and in the third grade.
College has always been an important
dream that would come true...if you
could just manage the grades.

Now you are a senior, after eleven
plus years of work and study, the great
day is in sight.

Or was, until that bright red truck
pulled in front of your car. Now you
lay sleeping...not here...yet not
there. There is no way of knowing what
you are feeling or thinking, if anything. But, my darling, the threshold
is still there. You are still eighteen.

When you awaken, and you will, it will
be here, to the life we know, or...
the great life that is ahead for all
of us. Whichever, I know you will face
it with the dignity and sweetness with
which you have always faced everything.

Longfellow wrote: "I pass through
this world but once. Any good therefore that I can do for my fellow man,
let me do it now. Let me not defer it
nor neglect it, for I shall not pass
this way again."

I am proud, my dearest, that I
shared and benefited from your love and
I apologize for taking it for granted.
I know now, even the smallest flower
should be appreciated while it is
here, for if it were not for us, it
would not exist at all.

Your Sister

Petar Sardelich

BILL BLINN

CLOUDY NIGHT

No one cares how much clouds weigh and there is a sizable school of thought that doesn't care. I am presently lying in the grass in the backyard of Susie Folgate and she does care, which means I care, too. Susie wears what were once called pedal pushers. They are pretty girl pink and somewhat snug. I care a great deal, the more I think about it. I am not in love with Susie Folgate. That came way later.

The grass was soft, though not as soft as Susie Folgate, but life, I realized at age fourteen, often worked out that way. We were studying the passage of the nighttime clouds, which was Susie's idea as to why we should be lying out there in the moonlight, I had a different rationale in mind.

"How high do you think they are?" Susie said.

"The clouds? Miles, probably."

There was a silence, then Susie Folgate said, "Bobby Fox and Shirley Gossage went skinny dipping last weekend."

"Seriously?"

"You bet. Out to Palmers Quarrey."

"Who told you they went skinny dipping?"

"Bobby Fox, naturally. Girls never tell about things like that."

"Look. Look up there."

"That skinny white line? Is that what I'm looking at?"

"It's a contrail, is what that is. A contrail."

She propped herself up on one elbow. "And what the dickens is a contrail?"

"It's like the wake on a motorboat. It's what a jet plane leaves behind."

She turned, presenting her back to him. "I feel all wet back there. Do I have leaves and grass on the back of my blouse?"

"Let me look. Yeah. There's a bunch of stuff."

"Oh, my mom will slay me!" Her voice underwent a change as she tried to sound like her mother. "Young lady, what have you been doing? You have no business rolling around in the wet grass! Certainly not with some raggedy boy!"

"Stand still! Let me brush you off!"

"Double hockey sticks! She will slay me alive! She'll send me to the home for the unwed."

"Stand still, damnit!"

"Don't you damnit me, Mister Man! My mom will absolutely—"

"For God's sake, shut up about your mom!"

"Shame on you! Just shame on you!"

"Oh, don't cry...please don't cry... Oh, Jesus Christ, please don't—"

"I'll cry if I want to, darn it!"

"Oh, for Christ's sake..."

"And you can just stop taking the Lord's name in vain, Mister!"

"You've still got leaves and grass on your butt."

"Stop that! Stop touching me!"

"I'm just trying to—"

"You're just trying to cop a feel is what you're—"

Her hand lifted, her index finger pointed towards the clouds. "Oh, dear God," she said.

"I stopped, I stopped!"

"Not that, I know you stopped. But look! There's another one!"

"Another what?"

She pointed her head in a new direction. "One of those thingamabobs you told me about before. A convair."

"Contrail."

"Whatever. One of those thingamabobs ..."

He let the night enfold them both. "Those big jets can go a long way."

"How far?"

He gave it some thought. He looked at her closely. "You're in a weird mood."

She looked to the gathering clouds.

"My mom and dad are going to get a divorce. They told us last night at supper."

He tried to think of something to say. Nothing presented itself. He put his arm around her. She neither welcomed that or pulled away. They stood in her dew drenched backyard for a long time looking up at the clouds as their future sailed off into a darkness they could not understand.

The moon was their memory.

DEAR MISTER HARDY

Dear Mister Hardy:

There is a picture of you in the corridor at the Motion Picture facility. I always address it as I pass by, "Hello, Oliver," but I hesitate using that in this letter as we have never met and I am aware of the fact that you are on a screen.

Slightly formal when meeting new people as in: "I am Mister Hardy and this is my dear friend, Mr. Laurel." The fact that your picture has never responded to my greeting tells me I must avoid taking liberties when addressing you.

The name of the movie is "Way Out West" and it concerns you and Mister Laurel travelling through cowboy country as you seek to right a wrong that has come to our attention. Then as the film progressed we followed you and Mister Laurel to the porch of the saloon where the soundtrack introduced the irresistible bass baritone, Chill Wills, offering his version of "Commence to Dancin'" in his own style and manner. It's a simple song with a

simple melody and shortly thereafter
you and Mister Laurel were dancing a
simple soft shoe. No explanation, no
reason. Just two men entranced by the
melody and taking advantage of the
situation.

You are a large man who brings considerable size and poundage to the
dance floor, but the grace and lightness
afoot were an utter delight for the
viewer. This viewer especially.

As the years went on, I would occasionally ask myself, why I was so taken
with you. You were, after all, half
of a comedy team, a famous one to be
sure. There were those who lined up as
fans of Mister Laurel. Deeding to him
greater creative input that they would
give to you, but I simply accepted that
reality, even while secretly wondering
why I was so taken with you.

Until Diane spoke up, that is.

Diane was the love of my thirteen-
year-old life and libido. (At age thirteen, these things are inseparable.)

Still. I was erect and smitten one
day when we were seated in the empty
football stadium actually having a conversation, with me telling Diane of my
odd fixation on Oliver Hardy, when she
offered her take on it, which was simply: "Your dad is kind of chunky, too."

And there it was, a rock solid truth
from mini-skirted Diane, which sent me

racing away to my home, no easy choice, given the cut of that mini skirt, I assure you.

In my living room, I took down my dad's picture from the mantle, then raced down the stairs to the tape machine where the copy of "Way Out West" was kept. I slammed the tape home and hit the "play" button.

The image fluttered onto the screen at once.

There he was, and I could immediately see the resemblance between my dad and Mister Hardy as he led the horse across the stream near the traditional Western cowboy town. It wasn't that they could have been brothers, they were identical.

I was overcome with a sense of dread as they reached the saloon and Mister Hardy looking so much like my dad, mounted the steps to the saloon and the gentle bass of Chill Wills was once again heard, "Commence to dancing, Commence to Prancin'...."

A trademark Kewpie Doll smile on Hardy's face as the dance went on.

I miss that grin more than words can say.

On second thought, the words you are hearing are trying to do just that.

I knew he was going to kill me, I knew it from the moment he walked into the 7-Eleven. The skinny kid in the yellow windbreaker was going to kill me.

I had never seen him before, but I knew. His right hand moved back to the empty windbreaker pocket. When it came out, it was no longer empty. Now it gripped a metallic object that was a cold blue. It was manufactured by a company called Smith & Wesson and it held six fully lethal thirty-eight cal-iber pistol shells in its chambers. My voice came out higher than I would have preferred.

"Jesus!" I said.

Our eyes met then and his mouth worked as he seemed to search for words. But before he spoke, his weapon barked a dull sound, rendering his words irrelevant. There was a period of confusion and chaos and someone could be heard starting to sob. That is about the time I started to recognize my own voice in a state of mounting whimper.

I was lying on the 7-Eleven floor. It was cool and oddly comforting. I heard a woman's voice telling the listener on

the other end that someone was bleeding
like a slaughtered pig. My hand pat-
ted my fat belly and I found it both
moist and warm. I was afraid I had wet
myself. Then I realized that wasn't
true. My hand came away grimly crimson.

I was slowly starting to realize I
was bleeding out.

One of the teenage female clerks
proudly proclaimed that she had called
911 and paramedics were on the way. I
lifted a hand to show I understood.
Then I noticed the hand was red with my
blood and the fear within me escalated
sharply. The shirt over my ample belly
was wet and warm. I coughed up a delicate plume of crimson cloud.

Jesus God. I was dying.

A beefy man with a florid face
inserted himself into my field of
vision. I could not hear him, but from
the popping veins in his face I could
tell he was yelling.

"Are you Catholic?" was the repeated
phrase. It was paired up with, "Do you
want me to call a priest?"

The last part brought me to the dark
awareness that he thought I was dying,
there on the cold tile of the 7-Eleven.

Then there was the oncoming darkness. Not the darkness of a shadow or
an approachable storm cloud. It was a
darkness made palpable, a darkness with
a taste to it, a bitter and sad taste.

The sadness was my death.

Then I spoke up, weakly to be sure, but I did manage to eke out the fact that I was going to turn down a chance to indulge in an additional helping of frosty darkness. No more for me, thank you.

I have had my fill. No more for me.

I did not savor the taste of this darkness. I would not get inside it either

START OF NEW FALL

Her name was Taffy. She was a rust-colored cocker spaniel. I loved her more than my next breath. I was six and had just discovered that skipping was a much faster method of moving than running. There was more breeze and freedom to skipping and all six-year-olds knew that.

I would skip from the time I left the school bus until I reached the starting point of my home's driveway. The chirp of my Keds alerted Taffy to my return and she matched my charge with one of her own. This reunion was the high point of our day.

It was autumn, a chilly and golden time, a time filled with new items that needed to be dealt with by Taffy. First and foremost with the new horse bought into our lives by the iceman. He arrived once a week, driving an old red wagon loaded with fifty-pound chunks of ice, the wagon pulled by an aging horse who all the kids fed with weeds from the nearest vacant lot. The dumb-eyed horse chewed loudly, causing Taffy to leap in a distracting manner, though in no way threatening. When you are a funny cocker spaniel, you don't threaten an ice wagon horse. The horse would occasionally glance at Taffy like a side dish he had not ordered. Taffy did not stop jumping. Taffy started to whine and whimper when we gave the horse a mouthful of weeds. The driver of the ice wagon was Bert and he had biceps the size of a new jeep. He kept telling Taffy to shut the hell up. Taffy kept right on wagging.

The following Tuesday, there was no reunion with Taffy, which meant Mom or my sister had given her a treat.

I went into the house and made a baloney sandwich on white Wonder bread and went into the laundry room. And that's where I found Taffy lying on the floor.

She was motionless and her belly was not moving. Her rust colored fur was cold. That's when I heard my sister crying in the living room. I sniffed and stroked Taffy's tummy.

I didn't know my sister loved Taffy that much.

When I got to the living room I found my sister on the phone. Her mascara was a smear under her eyes. "Did you hear about Daddy?" she said.

"No," I said "What are you talking about?"

She murmured a soft goodbye into the phone. She put the receiver on the hook, "He's in University Hospital" she said.

"Is he okay?"

She was motionless, then her head moved back and forth and again back and forth.

Then the dumb part of me arrived and I said "Taffy's in the laundry room."

"What?"

"Taffy's in the laundry room."

She moved toward the kitchen, mouth wide open as she looked at me. "The dog? You're talking about your fucking dog?"

I nodded obediently.

She went on her way, shaking her head. "Jesus, are you mental?" And she went into the kitchen. Her footsteps sounded from the laundry room, "Oh, Taffy!" I heard her cry out. "Oh, poor baby!"

And that's how I lost the two best listeners in my family. I miss them both and think of them often.

THE MAGIC OF THE BLUE DRESS

He intended to write something profound, something that would be unexpected from one whose stock in trade
was car chases and western quick-draw
shootouts.

He knew he was capable of writing
something insightful, something profound, and he fully intended to write
it after getting a coffee at Starbucks.
He would go back to his place and think
about the ocean and the universe and
that's the kind of thought that would
generate the kind of insightful writing
that would convince people he ought to
be writing for Nova.

It was in him somewhere; he was sure
of it.

He was in line at Starbucks, his mind
adrift as he searched for a profound
treasure with which he could establish
himself as a deep thinker, a man who
could slice through the nonsense and
demonstrate his superior intellect.

He was staring at the painting on
the wall, a seascape, as he was convinced that bathing his brain in images
of size and power would generate the
kind of deep thinking that had evaded

him in all these years of pulp platitudes.

A woman edged into line in front
of him, her smile asking permission.
He nodded, stepping back to allow her
entry. A silent and civilized give and
take. Well-suited to a man thinking
deep thoughts of gritty insight.

The woman was in her early thirties
and her addition to the line added a
floral scent, a pleasant plus, it seemed
to the insight-seeker.

His look drifted from the seascape
and held momentarily on her backside as
she took her place in front of him.

Her dress was blue, teal blue, and
he wondered about her eyes. Women often
dressed with the goal of matching wardrobe with anatomy, after all, and he
liked that.

He prized his gaze away from her
backside and returned his look to the
seascape once more. It seemed to him
that the crashing waves there had
become endowed with soft and appeal-
ing curves. The color of the surf was a
pleasant teal blue.

The motion of the waves had slowed
somehow into seductive serenade. He was
confused about the mammoth insight he
had sought, it seemed to be superseded
by sexual meanderings, he turned away,
closed his eyes.

He breathed in a deep breath,

seeking calm. Fantasies of prime
buttocks had little to do with seeking
of deep philosophy. Trim teal skirts
were outside the goal.

The line moved and the Teal Lady
was at the counter where the smiling barista waited. She was a regular she called her by name. Her name
was "Marla." It had a good fit, and he
approved. Marla, the lady in teal. Good
sound. Good butt. Good combo.

The profound insight would not show
itself. He stood at the door of the
Starbucks for a long time, looking out
at the teal blue vision moving off into
the distance. He let his brain bumble
along for a moment, but nothing profound popped up to fill the empty space
there,

A couple of late arrivals shoulder
bumped him and by the time he
re-established himself and was once
again facing the window, the target
of teal was no longer in sight. As
absent as the so-called profound and
insightful thought.

And so it came to him as slowly as
melting spring snow. He had truly never
had a thought that could be classified
as profound.

Clever, yes. Quick, to be sure. But
not profound.

That was saved for the reality that
he had never climbed that particular

hill. He had posed and postured there, but never reached the peak, save for this last realization.

He was hoping Marla would understand.

He went home and took a nap, then set about writing a new car chase.

THUNDER

I suppose, had there been an inno-
cent onlooker to my move, he might have
described it as being an aimless move.
But there was nothing aimless about it.

I was drawn to the lightning and the
rumble that was its accompaniment as
surely as a firefly finds its way to the
Boy Scout's flashlight's beam. There was
a helplessness to my move, one I could
neither define nor control. The lightning changed the texture and color of
the boulders serving as the backdrop,
turning them to an angry cauliflower—a
mutant madness that had to be dealt
with. The thunder created a concussive
force that thumped against my chest. I
leaned forward against these oncoming
blows, fighting their force as best I
could.

My best was not good enough. I stood
unmoving, lost in the moment, a moment
that plundered the sunlight from its
giddiness. I was wrapped in a blanket
of fearful knowledge. A knowledge that
told me it was time to huddle beneath
the blanket one last time—that mercy
was revealed. Its time done. That the
stones were about to find their voice

and that their battle cry would shred
the sunshine.

I tried to awaken, but could not.
Sorry. You had to be there.

I am addicted to thunderstorms. The
deep bass rumble triggers something in
me, a lusting after ungoverned power. A
need to experience something not polit-
ically correct. A sound that resonates
from one canyon wall to another. Not a
polite thing. Nothing reasonable.

Thunderstorms are there to remind us
of our wounded spirit.

As one born and raised in the rolling flatlands of Ohio, the word moun-
tain was reserved for seriously overweight professional wrestlers. So, when
the family moved to Utah, my education
entered a new and more serious phase.

Mountains were everywhere, majestic
and astonishing, poking the imagination
with an urgent need, demanding action
that must be paid.

Writing about our past doesn't "put it to bed." It wakes it up.

MAGGIE MALOOLY

HOW I FOUND MY SASS

Las Vegas, Nevada

"Well, what's the matter wit ya, anyway? You one of those dames that won't put out? You frigid or something?"

That did it. I stood up, left him sitting at the table in the dining room and took the elevator up to my room in the MGM Hotel.

Once inside, outraged by his crude sophomoric remarks, caught between anger and derision, I rested my head against the door. Eyes closed, I tried to calm myself. Why did this man, one I had just met, assume a few hours of social conversation would automatically assure a sexual encounter? Believe I would give way to his persistence? Insist he be allowed to come to my room? Worse, why would he feel he had the right to question my sexuality?

Earlier in the evening, in the casino, I was feeding a hungry and unyielding slot machine. At the slot machine next to me, a man was as unsuccessful as I with the one arm bandit he was nourishing. We began to commiserate about our bad luck. Finally, donating the last of my quarters to the charitable foundation for casino owners, I rose.

"Have you ever tried Keno?" he asked.

"No," I replied, "I'm not a dedicated gambler. My sister and I came to Vegas to see the shows."

"Well, you might have better luck at Keno. Come with me, I'll show you how to play."

After his brief instruction, I bought several Keno cards and, surprisingly, won four hundred dollars. Flush with my unexpected windfall, I offered to buy the man dinner in the hotel's restaurant.

The dinner was good, the conversation social. Then, along with our last cup of coffee, came the pitch. Subtle innuendos at first, and then this male animal, believing himself irresistible, grew more persistent, seemingly unaware, heedless of my gentle, polite and, finally, downright refusal. Just what part of NO didn't he understand?

Now, mumbling in my hotel room, I hurled out all the angry words I hadn't spoken. "Look, fellow, I invited you to dinner, not me!" Yeah, that's a good one. How 'bout, "Did it ever occur to you that sexually you're a zero?"

Slowly, as I exhausted all the insults I could think of, I sensed something else. Deep within, I was disappointed in myself. Why did I tolerate that behavior from a man? This wasn't the first time a man was out of bounds and behaved nastily when not successful? I thought about it. I wondered if I were complicit in his repugnant behavior?

When this would-be Lothario crudely insisted on sex and resorted to insults, I played the traditional female role. I was conciliatory, demurring, tolerating. I relinquished my control over the situation. And I am not the only woman who has done so.

Women, single, married, widowed, divorced, complain to each other about this embarrassing, annoying, hurtful, sometimes threatening element in our lives.

A friend of mine, in the throes of an emotional divorce, told about receiving telephone calls from casual male acquaintances, even one from a neighbor's husband. Their message was always the same. "Now that you no longer have a husband, I'd be willing to help fill your sexual needs." In truth, that was the last thing she had in mind.

Rationalizations abound for men behaving inappropriately. Boys will be boys, so what's all the fuss about? Just sowing their wild oats. Just love women.

Through the ages, women have been conditioned traditionally, religiously and socially, to tolerate unsolicited and offensive conduct from men. We should be flattered, complimented, pleased to be noticed.

At Catholic school, the nuns instructed us to respect all of God's children. Without question a noble posture, but I wasn't given any ABCs on dealing with ungodly aggression from boys and men.

So, I, along with my sisters, have been conditioned to silently endure the practice of men who whistle, catcall, leer, grab and make crude remarks about our bodies.

This hasn't worked well for women. We feel helpless and forced to bear it. Even worse, we're blamed as the instigators of criminal sexual assault. How long will we tolerate this?

"Not anymore!" I promised my hotel room. "That was the very last time any man insults me and gets away with it."

With that stalwart resolve, I set on a new path allowing, no, demanding, only the utmost respect from men.

At the time, I didn't know how assertive I would become. I didn't know how empowering it would be.

A LESSON FOR LIFE

We raced home to tell our mom all about the Saturday matinee we just saw starring my favorite cowboy, Bob Steele. I liked his blue eyes and the white hat he always wore and because he always saved someone and always got the bad guys.

On the way home, my brother, Tommy, my sister, Eileen and I picked which one of us would be the good guy, the bad guy and the funny old guy.

My mom loved to watch us act out the whole movie for her. At least, we thought she did. She'd stop whatever she was doing, sit on the living room couch and laugh at our version of the movie. Because I was nine, the oldest of four, I had first choice. Bob Steele. Tommy, eight, was next in line but he was very shy, so he always played the musical comb. And he would only play the comb if he could sit behind the couch, hidden from view, as he hummed out his version of a cowboy tune.

Eileen, six, could pick whatever part was left. She never wanted to play the lady because the lady had nothing to do except be scared. She picked the funny guy, Gabby Hayes. With the cast set, the three of us bolted through the kitchen door, past the dining room and into the living room of our apartment

Mom was sitting in the living room, holding my little brother, Ronnie, on her lap. He was four. Our favorite. He had golden brown curls all over his head. He looked just like a picture of the Baby Jesus that my teacher, Sister Mary Theresa, had on her classroom wall.

Next to my mom sat a stranger. Mr. Navin. Our father. Where did he come from? Why was he here? Something was wrong, very wrong. Without her usual smile, my mom looked strained.

Was he coming back to live with us again? I hate the thought. I don't like him. He has already come and gone a few times before. Just left without even a "see ya." I vowed I would never ever call him Dad. Real dads don't just go and leave their children.

"Kids," my mom said, "your father and I have something to tell you. It's very important. We saw a doctor yesterday, a very special doctor."

I held my breath. My mom was never without a smile, a laugh, fun, except when we kids did something stupid. This was not good

"You know how Ronnie falls and can't get up without our help?"

Yes, we knew. When he was about two years old, our baby brother started to trip and fall. At first, it was only once in a while but then it was more often. When we all ran around playing games in our apartment, Ronnie fell a lot. Then he'd get up and start running again.

We used to laugh and say, "You're tripping over your own two feet." Mom's sister, Lilly, said that Ronnie's balance was off because he still had his baby curls. Lilly said to take him to the barber and once Ronnie had a real boy haircut, he'd get his strength back. Even as young as I was, I thought she sounded goofy.

My mom took Ronnie to many doctors, but they said it was just growing pains, nothing to worry about. But, we could see he was getting worse, falling more often.

By the time, Ronnie was four, he no longer was able to stand up without help. It was routine for us to pick him up, stand him on his feet and wait a second or two to see if his balance held. Once he was steady, we'd run on. My mom grew more troubled. She took him to more doctors hoping to find answers.

Now, seeing Mr. Navin sitting there, I was scared. Something bad was happening. My mom held Ronnie closely. Something was very bad.

"Kids," my mom said, "this special doctor examined Ronnie and says he knows what is wrong. He told us that Ronnie is going to get worse."

Oh, no, not my Baby Jesus brother. He's so sweet, so good, never whines. It can't be. We'll pray to God and Ronnie will get better. I know he will.

My mom said, "The doctor told us we should take care of Ronnie. Make him happy and watch over him."

I heard what she said; I saw her face, her sadness, the pain she held over what was in store for him.

I didn't look at Mr. Navin. I knew he would never stay. He would never be there for my mom, Ronnie or us. He would never ever be a factor in our lives. Who cares? We always get by each time he disappears. We don't need him. And, just as I knew he would, he left a week or so later. It was fine with me. My mom was all we needed.

In retrospect, I now realize this was the day that changed all of our lives. From that time, our focus would always be Ronnie first; everything and everyone else would be second. Ronnie would be our priority, our daily prayer for him to get better.

As we grew a bit older, we were told more of the terrible suffering my brother would endure. He had Muscular Dystrophy, the Duchenne type. Soon he began to walk on his toes, stomach protruding to maintain his balance, falling often and lying there until someone picked him up.

When Ronnie was about eight years old, my brother, Tom, lifted him up and put him in a wheelchair. He never walked again.

We became a family with one goal: keep Ronnie happy and alive until there was a cure. And, Ronnie became our precious gift, as well as our responsibility. Our love and hope for him taught us selflessness, patience, kindness, understanding and watchfulness for Ron's growing needs.

Tom and my Mom bore the brunt of the physical effort it took to care for Ronnie. For the rest of his life they dressed, undressed, fed, tended to his most intimate needs, lifted him into and out of bed and carried him on their backs when there was no wheelchair access. Over time the physical effort caused both of them to undergo spinal surgeries several times.

Then, the time came when it was necessary for my mom or Tom to sleep beside him to be just a breath away from his call. Relentlessly, they persevered.

Eileen and I had it easier. We cared for Ron during the day. We fed him, brought what he asked for and did silly things to entertain him when Tom and my Mom were at work. And though we never discussed it, we felt deep despair as we witnessed the gradual wasting away of his body: the loss of the use of his arms, muscle strength, the weakening of his lungs, the attacks on his stalwart heart, even the ability to laugh out loud. We all marveled at his inner strength. He never asked why me? Never once complained, even when we forgot to get him something he asked for.

Ronnie handled the failure of his body with enduring fortitude. One day he told my mom how sorry he felt for Jack, his new friend at school. Months earlier, Jack was a high school basketball star. Polio left him in a wheelchair unable to ever walk again.

My mom said, "Honey, why are you so sad about him?"

"Mom," he said, "Jack could walk and run before. I don't remember what it was like to walk and run. I don't miss it like he does."

Once, I overheard my mom consoling another mother whose child was mentally impaired. The woman told my mom how sorry she was to see Ronnie so incapacitated. My mom replied, "Oh, it's much harder for you. My boy can say, Mom, I love you. You'll never have that joy."

Unjustly, Ronnie died in an iron lung several weeks after an emergency tracheotomy. He was in total isolation behind a glass window. For the first time in his life, one of us wasn't beside him. It was unfair after all he had lived through.

Tom was inconsolable. My mom was lost for a long time. Ronnie had been the center of our lives. Our days circled around his needs. It had been a long and tough battle for Ronnie and for us.

If given the opportunity, would we do it again? Absolutely.

Ronnie was our gift, our angel.

QUESTIONING

Was I a good mom? Yes. Did I make mistakes? Yes. Was I bewildered? Yes. Frustrated? Yes. At my wit's end? Yes. Did I always know what to do? No. Did I always understand? No. But, now, now years after the job is done, now, I know. I know.

When one disobeys, I wouldn't shout, "Go to your room." Now I would say, "Wait a minute, this isn't like you, what's the matter, what's bothering you?"

When I hear one say, clutching his dog, "At least you'll always love me," I would go to him, hug him and tell him, "I always love you, I always will."

I wish I had been better at understanding my children. I wish I had known what to say when they were uncertain. I wish I knew when they were troubled and needed encouragement.

I wish they always knew, even when I goofed, that I still loved them more than anything in life.

I wish. I wish.

I wish I could do it all over again.

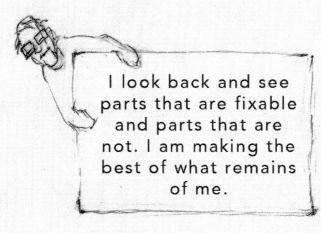

I look back and see
parts that are fixable
and parts that are
not. I am making the
best of what remains
of me.

JOAN TANNEN

Jim . . .
   Was my boyfriend, but not at first.

When I drove onto the MPTF campus in a U-Haul truck with my furniture in back and my cat, Alex, in his crate beside me, I made an unintentional, grand entrance. I mashed against another resident's car as I parked the truck. Having to do first things first, I left everything and hurried to the Country House to confess my sin. The first person I saw was Beverly—whom I had already met. She was with her friend Jim. She rallied the troops in the persons of Chris (maintenance) and Miguel (hospitality) who came to extricate the truck away from the other car without further damage, and, of course, many other people gathered around to gaff the situation. This group included the couple whose car I had damaged with me promising them to make good on the damage. This was my introduction to MPTF, and I finally moved in.

I moved to the campus in mid-December and the first of many holiday parties took place almost as soon as I arrived. Not knowing anybody at first, I gravitated to Beverly and Jim. Beverly was a cute, hyper little gal—full of energy. She ran the poker game and if you wanted to get into a sports pool, Beverly was the one to go to. Jim had arrived about six months before I did. He played poker, and she swept him into her poker circle. and they soon became a couple and continued to be for about three more years. Jim was in the beginning stages of Parkinson's Disease. He had had to give up flying his own plane when his depth perception was compromised, and a few other symptoms appeared. He decided then and there to come to MPTF. Beverly was good for Jim. She got him to go to exercise and nagged at him to swing his arms and keep mobile. We were all in exercise class together. As the years went by, Beverly discovered that a bad blood transfusion had left her with symptoms of hepatitis C. As it progressed, she drifted away from Jim, although they were still friends, and toward her family. With her family around her, she succumbed to her illness.

Several months passed and one day my phone rang. It was Jim. "Would you like to go to the movie with me?" he invited. He took me completely by surprise.

I mumbled, "S-sure, okay. Shall I meet you at the theater?"

I never imagined myself with Jim. He was a good looking guy with pretty but sad blue eyes. Up close he had eyelashes that any girl would give her eye teeth for—long and lush—but, after all, I had known Jim always as part of a couple. His call came out of left field, but, as he confessed to me later, he had had a crush on me almost from the start. Nothing momentous happened on our first date, but he asked me to go to the next movie and to everything else together, and, what do you know, we fell in love. We went on our first date on February 1 and not quite two months later on his birthday, March 24, I wrote this poem to him:

> Why can't we keep our hands off each other?
> It's so unseemly.
> When we walk together why do our hands
> Snap together like magnets on a fridge?
> Why do our eyes seek each other across a room?
> Why can't I keep the silly grin off my face whenever I see you?
> We're in our twilight years and here we are
> Acting like a couple of teenagers
> Do people snicker behind their hands when they see us
> because we had the nerve to fall in love at our age?
> My dear, it's so unseemly!

One lovely summer afternoon, as a soft breeze drifted in the window filled with the scent of jasmine, we were making love when a loud knock shattered the stillness. We looked in horror as the door opened and in walked the laundry lady with my fresh clothes, a day earlier than they were supposed to be here. Suffice to say, we were caught "flagrante delicto." I'm sure there was a lot of chatter in Spanish that afternoon in the laundry room. I can never see that woman that she doesn't give me a sly, little smile as if to say, "I'll never tell, but I know . . . I know . . ."

We were in that delicious stage for about two years and then our ages and Jim's Parkinson's gradually slowed us down. Our passionate kisses became affectionate little pecks. Jim started falling a lot. He never broke any bones, but he was covered in bruises. I came down with shingles, which played a tune on me, and then had a hip replacement. We both ended up with walkers. We couldn't hold hands while walking down the lane together anymore, because we had to hold onto our walkers.

Jim came over every evening to watch television with me. As he left to go home to the Villa, we would always kiss each other goodnight, and, unsteady as we both were, invariably, we would fall into my closet. After two such episodes, Brenda told us to be careful because she was running out of that type of closet door.

Finally, Jim ended up in the hospital, J-Wing. He went on to rehab and had to stay there for a while because he was now ready for long-term care. They had not had a bed for him there, and then they did. He wanted to go back to the Villa so badly. They promised him an electric wheelchair, but it wasn't quite ready, whereby he could go back and forth every day.

One night, I'd gone to a jazz concert at LACMA, and I had just gotten home when the phone rang. It was the social worker from Long Term. Jim had just died of a heart attack. He had died instantly just after he had gone to bed. He was free now of all the pain and suffering.

We had loved each other for six years, and now, as I grieved for him, I imagined him flying freely off into the hereafter in his beloved airplane and dipping his wings as he passed over our campus.

MY DAD

I've been lonely all my life for my father who died much too young for him—late thirties—and decidedly so for three-year-old me and six-year-old brother, Danny. He died before I was old enough to really get to know him, but I feel in my heart that I loved him very much. After he left us, there remained in my life a terrible, empty void that nothing seemed to fill. I wasn't really aware of what it was or why. It was just there.

I have a vivid memory of the day Daddy came home very sick from a business trip. It seemed unseemly that it was a beautiful, spring day. In the following days, people were bustling in and out of his bedroom, and of the house, otherwise, being very quiet. Danny and I were often cautioned to not make any noise.

One sunny day, the door to his bedroom was open. I had been longing to see my Daddy, but he wasn't there. I thought he must be playing a game with me. I looked under the bed, in the closet and in every corner, but he wasn't there. Nobody seemed to notice my small predicament. Mom was unavailable . . . people talked quietly in small groups . . . We—Danny and I—were told to be brave and not pester Mom . . . She was very, very sad . . . Danny was older than I, but he couldn't tell me what was going on either. And, nobody ever really explained to us what was happening. We didn't even get a chance to say goodbye. We were thought to be too young and, therefore, we weren't expected to grieve at our tender ages, but we did.

Mom went through a very, traumatic time after his death. After a long bout of grieving, including a nervous breakdown, she finally got on with her life. We were in the midst of the Depression, and she worried about getting her teaching career back and worried especially about losing our home. She worked so hard, taking any substitute job she could until she could get back to a permanent teaching job. I was a problem. Danny had already started school, but I was too young to be there. I got shuffled about to one person or another while she was teaching, usually my grandparents or our nextdoor neighbor.

Over the years I sometimes yearned to ask Mom about Daddy, but I always sensed that it would make her unbearably sad and would break down the walls that she had so carefully erected.

I wished always that we could have talked more about Daddy than we did.

Except in occasional vague references to him, she never talked about him to Danny and me. We just moved on, but did we really? We were all in our little cones of loneliness. If we had sat down and reminisced about him and how much we loved him and missed him, we would be together in our solitude.

Sometimes, close friends of the family would mention a little loving anecdote about him. For instance, he used to carry one or the other of us kids around on his shoulders, singing "Ragtime Cowboy." I hungered to hear any such stories, but I was too shy to ask for more. In that era, nobody talked about death or the person who died.

Not having a father was such a big hole in my life but one that I couldn't seem to put my finger on. I needed him so much. I needed him to show me who I was or what I could be, because I don't think I was ever sure.

You'd think that would open up a communication between Mom and me, but I don't think it occurred to her. She just said something like, "That's nice, dear." That probably sounds insensitive on her part, but people were very private about their feelings at that time.

Both Danny and I needed the confidence that only a father can give to his children. We needed to feel that our Dad knew, without a doubt, that we would grow up to be fulfilled, happy human beings who would be able to do anything in life that we desired. He never got a chance to teach us how to play sports or to be a good sport . . . to let us both know that we could be and do anything in life that we wanted.

Danny, certainly Danny, needed a Dad, to throw balls to him, yes, but to teach him how to grow up to be a man. He needed a Dad to teach him with patience so many new things and to grow up to be the best man that he could be.

I wish he could have been there to console me when a boy I liked didn't pick me to dance with him in dancing class. I'm sure he would have comforted me by telling me I must have been the prettiest girl there, and what did that silly boy know? I envied my friends. They all had fathers.

When I was around nine or ten years old, I wrote what I called my novel with pictures. It was about a father and his young daughter. The father was very ill, and the ten-year-old daughter went to work in an office (doing I don't know what) to take care of him. They were very poor and lived in a small tenement in a slum. It was very soap opera-ish, but it was my first writing effort of any length.

It was all about my father.

CAPE COD IS MY HEART

Cape Cod, a long spit of land that curves out into the Atlantic Ocean, is a mecca for artists who are drawn to its purity of light and who keep trying to capture its essence.

Cape Cod is a palette of colors, bright and also subtle . . . ultramarine blues of every shade in its skies and bays and its blueberry bushes . . . pale, yellow ochre sand of its beaches . . . weathered, gray houses like silvery gray driftwood, changing to charcoal after the rain . . . the subtle gray-green ground cover and foliage, such as bayberry and scrub pine poking up through the sand and fighting for survival against the ever-constant wind . . . the alizarin crimson cranberry bogs . . . the flaming orange-reds, pinks, lavenders and yellows of sunsets that inspire awe. This is one part of Cape Cod.

I love Cape Cod in every sensory part of my soul . . . the smells, tastes, sounds and sights of Cape Cod . . . the pungent scents of pine and bayberry . . . the comforting crackle and smell of wood smoke in the fireplace after an afternoon swim in the ocean . . . the taste and aroma of fish, clam chowder and of fried clams . . . the smells of popcorn and baking bread on trips into town. All of these things are parts of why I cherish Cape Cod.

I love the sea at any time and place . . . I love the crump—his sound of the waves braking on the shore . . . I love the typical, austere architecture of New England . . . the homey, rose-covered cottages of weathered gray wood . . . I love the mournful sound of a lone trawler chugging out into Lewis Bay, clanging all the way . . . I love the sound of the wind soughing though the pine trees . . . the slight, slapping sound of sails on a tack . . . I love the curious way voices travel over the sand flats across a distance when the tide is out.

I love its history—Cape Cod was the first landfall of the pilgrims on the *Mayflower*. I love the Cape from Woods Hole, where oceanographers hang out to study the fish of the sea, to the tip of Provincetown—P-town, as the natives call it, with its artsy atmosphere . . . the Pilgrim Tower . . . Race Point where the water is so clear and cold you can see every pebble on the bottom even when swimming in water over your head. I love Hyannis where I spent many a summer, and I love the sailing camp at Wellfleet where I spent two of the happiest summers of my childhood. I love Dennis for the Cape Playhouse and Cinema with its mural by famous artist Rockwell Kent.

But, most of all, Cape Cod, Massachusetts, is a state of mind and spirit. I have loved everything about it to the very depths of my heart and soul for the whole of my life.

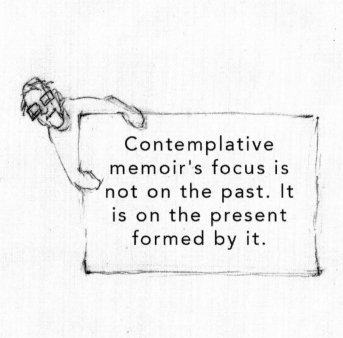

Contemplative memoir's focus is not on the past. It is on the present formed by it.

MIMI COZZENS

THE PRICE OF A PHOTO

A three-quarter page advertisement on page eight of the *New Herald Tribune* on Monday, March 27th, 1944, read: "The war's unpublished casualty lists." Further down the page it continued: "'War Babies' will shock you. Attention, Mrs. America! This frightening true picture is happening all around you! Children kept in close confinement—chained to trailers, put behind chicken wire, hungry, dirty, often too miserable to cry." Alongside these words was a photo of a two-year-old with dirty face, arms and legs, wearing a torn dirty undershirt and a diaper, tears running down her cheeks from big, sad eyes in a round face surrounded by straight, matted hair. A crust of bread lay by her side.

The day that photo was taken, the child's hair was carefully wetted and combed straight from the beautiful blond curls she had, only minutes before. The undershirt, which not ten minutes earlier rested on her small child's frame under a freshly-starched, blue-stripped dress and white pinafore, was torn and dirtied, along with the child, by a photographer's assistant. He carefully arranged the crust of bread beside the child for maximum effect, as she was placed by our mother in front of a white backdrop.

This so-called "frightening true picture" was staged in a photographer's studio in New York City using a professional child model. That model was my baby sister and I was there to witness just how that picture was taken. When the photographer wanted my sister to cry, he took the baby bottle she clutched in her small hands, the last refuge of the real world she knew, now that she was stripped of clean outer garments, dirtied and sitting in what must have seemed so alien a world to her young eyes.

But she had such spirit. I always admired her for that, even at that age. Her eyes flared, her face became defiant and she looked to our

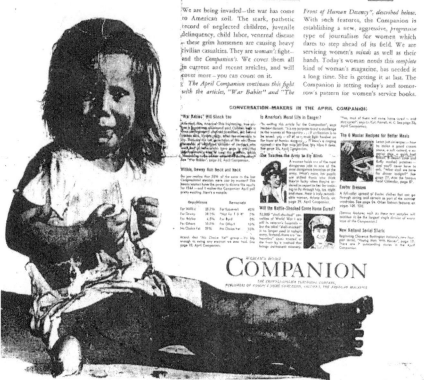

mother as if to say, "Hey, that big man just took my bottle away; tell him to give it back to me!"

My mother simply stood stock still and then very slowly crossed her muscular arms in front of the ample breasts of her five-foot-two broad frame. Her heart may have cracked a little underneath her navy polka-dot jersey dress from Montgomery Ward's latest catalogue, but her face never showed it. She did not smile. Her expression was stern, severe, and unyielding.

It was then that I watched my sister's spirits wane. She was no longer defiant; big tears welled up in her beautiful big blue eyes as she turned her gaze to look at the bottle, now resting on top of the camera. Fear and confusion looked out from those big eyes which seemed smaller now. I heard the click of the camera, the voice of the photographer saying: "Great, great, this is good, this is good." I knew that pleased my mother. And still she held her hardened stance. I knew why. It was the price she paid to keep my sister crying so they could get that picture. It was important to her that both her daughters were models, pleased the photographers, smiled for the camera, cried for the camera, got that good picture, got that five-dollar modeling fee—no small sum in 1944.

I was three and a half years old when I did my first modeling job. It was a Colgate Toothpaste ad. I looked out from long, red curls, wound around that same mother's fingers. I wore striped pajamas and a dark blue bathrobe, and asked the model/actor playing my father "What's bad breath, Daddy?" I had no idea what that meant or what I was doing. I just knew I could pretend this nice warm man was my daddy and he would be pleasant to me for as long as the camera clicked. And warmer than my own daddy had ever been, I thought. The people behind the camera told me how good I was at this new thing called modeling. I could emote in any way I was required to— smile, laugh, cry, look unhappy, sad, whatever was asked. They told her I was adorable and perfect at this business, a natural. This pleased my mother, and what little girl doesn't want to please her mother?

I became one of the most sought-after child models of the New York City advertising scene, as my mother liked to point out. I had the reputation of always coming through. There were times when I had as many as five jobs in one day. If another child model couldn't do the job right, got cranky or uncooperative, I'd be called in to finish the job.

I remember, late one day I was called onto the set of a life insurance ad where eight grown-up actor/models had been held up for hours on a complicated shoot. It was complicated because it required various attitudes and expressions from so many different people at the same time, and the child model they hired was uncooperative. I came in and finished the job in five minutes. I was not only a child model; I was a model child.

I liked all the attention I got from being a child model. It made up for all the attention I wasn't getting from my rather distant father at home. I didn't understand that at the time. That awareness came much later. But that day in 1944, as I stood watching those tears roll down my sister's cheeks, something clicked in my head along with the clicks of the camera I heard.

My sister was five weeks old when she did her first modeling job. She was registered at John Roberts Powers, New York's top modeling agency, before she was born. It was sort of a joke at the agency. The thought was if she or he was anything like her sister, the baby would be terrific in the business. I loved her very much. I thought she had come into my life to take the pressure away, to be my buddy, to save me. From what I wasn't sure.

I didn't get to go with my sister on very many of her modeling jobs, as I was either busy with my own or I had schoolwork. I call it schoolwork even though I wasn't attending school. I had a tutor and that mostly meant homework. I hated the isolation of homework. I was told my sister didn't take to modeling exactly as I had. She didn't want to sit still and was more interested, once she knew how, in roaming around the set doing what she wanted. Pretty smart, I thought. Why didn't I think of that? And after all, what were they complaining about? She was just a baby. I felt the need to stand up for her in a way I could never stand up for myself.

When my mother was busy with my sister, I learned to make the long trek from Queens to New York city by bus and subway by myself. I was seven and a half years old. I used to gaze out the window of the subway car and watch the imaginary track team I had created running out there along the third rail—the leaner, thinner boys up front, the fatties bringing up the rear. As I got older, I used to pretend they were losing weight for me.

That was my escape from the fear I felt. But at the time I never questioned. I just did it. Like the child who thinks all parents are just like hers, until she meets and gets to know her playmates' families. It was my life, the life my mother made for me, and I learned very early on to be the little adult it was necessary to be if you lived the life of a professional child.

The only time I remember disobeying my mother on a shoot was the time I was to pose in a bathtub full of bubble bath. The tub awaited my entrance. My mother forgot to bring an extra pair of underpants or anything else I might wear in the water, like trunks or a bathing suit. She insisted I get into the tub naked while she held up what seemed to me to be the skimpiest of towels, in a lame attempt to shield my four-year-old body from the cameraman and his assistants who were adjusting lights and camera angles within earshot and full view of what my mother was asking me to do. I was mortified. She insisted no one would know or care if I was naked once I was under all those bubbles. But I would know. I would care. Why wasn't that important? I knew they were going to have to keep recreating those bubbles. I'd watched them create the ones that were already there. They kept shaking their hands in the water as they poured in soap flakes and used an egg beater to keep the lather going and I knew they would continue to do that once I was in the tub, and for me to have that happen without the protection of those little, white, ruffled, cotton underpants terrified me.

Why couldn't she see that? In the end, I won. I stepped into that tub, my red curls piled atop my head, clutching my underpants stubbornly on me, as I kept my mother holding the towel around my upper half until I slipped beneath the bubbles. I didn't feel the temperature of the water or the bubbles that surrounded me, I only felt the embarrassment and shame at having made such a fuss in front of all those men. My mother paid the price of a new pair of underpants for me to wear home that night.

If my parents were not happy about something I'd done, all they had to do was look at me crooked and I would burst into tears. My sister was different from me. Stronger, I thought. Whenever I look at the so-called frightening "true picture" of the ad my sister did for the *Woman's Home Companion*, it is frightening to me all right, but I don't see a child kept in confinement, I see a two-year-old out in the world making a living. She wasn't chained to trailers. She was being trained to emote on cue. Not put behind chicken wire, more like on display. Not hungry for food, but for warmth and a kind word to protect her in an alien environment. Dirty, well yes, but I know just how that dirt came about. And, yes, certainly miserable enough to cry.

That particular day, I watched my sweet little sister learn something it would take me a lifetime to learn—how to turn the other cheek. From that day on, it would take a hell of a lot more than a crooked look to make her cry. The price of that particular photo.

My sister and I paid a heavy price for those photos we appeared in. I paid with my childhood. My sister remained a child for the rest of her life; but then, that's another story.

Autobiography lets your loved ones know you. Memoir lets your loved ones share you.

ALAN SLOAN

THE APARTMENT

In June of 1960, *The Apartment* starring Jack Lemon and Fred Mac-Murray premiered. The movie, directed by Billy Wilder, was an instant box-office hit and has become a comedy legend. After seeing the movie, Ben Mayo, my ex-roommate, and I jokingly considered suing the studio, Warner Brothers, for basing their movie on our lifestyle without our permission.

Ben and I had graduated City College in 1953 and because we were both 4-F we had begun to hang out together more often than we did during our undergraduate days. The summer and fall of 1953, we were both out of work and when we were not job searching, we spent some considerable time playing three-par golf on a course on Long Island. As our friendship deepened, we decided that when we both had jobs, and could afford it, we would get an apartment together in the "City."

It wasn't until 1955 that we were both making almost enough to afford an apartment in a decent Manhattan neighborhood. We weren't short by much, but it was going to be a stretch. We decided to forge ahead. We found a two-bedroom apartment on West 78th street between West End Avenue and Riverside Drive—just half a block from Riverside Park. The rent: $178 a month.

Ben's family owned a thriving dress manufacturing business in the Garment Center. Several months after our move to the city, Ben was visiting his father's office and ran into two salesman who were family friends. Richie Russo and Murray Hazan were in their late twenties, successful salesmen, well-spoken, well-dressed, and very successful womanizers. When Ben told them he had moved to the "City" and was living in a two-bedroom apartment their eyes lit up and then they proposed an "arrangement."

Their biggest problem was a place to entertain their dates. Hotel rooms were too obvious and too expensive. They would pay us what they would pay for a hotel room if we would leave the apartment for them to use one night a month after dinner. We would have to stay out until the late evening. There would be no "overnights." Ben said he thought it might work, would check with me, and get back to them.

Of course, we said yes. For us it was a no-brainer. This was an opportunity to get at least half our monthly rent paid with very little inconvenience. On that Thursday evening, Ben and I would either go our separate ways or, on occasion, meet for dinner and then see a Broadway show—or at least the second half of a Broadway show. We had learned from our City friends that you could join the returning first act intermission crowd, find an empty seat, and enjoy, at no cost, the rest of the play. For several years I was able to see a part of almost every Broadway production.

The arrangement worked very smoothly with one exception. One Thursday evening I returned home at the agreed upon "all clear" time. Much to my surprise I found a gorgeous, and very voluptuous, lady sitting alone in our living room. She was in tears. She had been left alone by her date who had told her to leave before 11:00 p.m. I sat down beside her to try to comfort her and the next thing I knew she was in my arms kissing me. I knew I was irresistible, but I didn't even know the lady. What should I do? I tried to figure out what was happening. I reached for her hand. It was hard and unyielding to my touch.

She pulled away from me and whispered "Don't be afraid. It's an artificial arm." I really don't remember much about the next fifteen minutes except I tried to reassure her that her disability made no difference to me. And then we were interrupted by the doorbell. Ben had returned. She managed to pull herself together and indicated it was time for her to leave. I phoned the doorman and asked him to get her a taxi. Handing me her phone number she left, asking me to call her. I assured her I would, but I never did. I was totally bewildered by the whole experience and she was much too complicated for me.

We never discussed that incident with Murray and Richie. They continued to use our place until Ben and I eventually moved to our own apartments. As single young men, we had many adventures in the years we were roommates and there are two more stories that really stand out.

It has to do with doctors and hospitals. Ben and I had been on the receiving end of numerous invitations to parties and gatherings "thrown" by friends and strangers. It became obvious that at some point we would have to reciprocate.

That meant thoroughly cleaning the apartment—floors, bathrooms, kitchen, etc, etc. A task that we had almost completely ignored until then. It took us two full days before the party to make the place presentable. It was dirty and sweaty work, but we persevered, and the party was a great success. The following day I woke up feeling unusually tired and weak. I knew it wasn't a hangover. When I used the john, I was horrified to see that my urine was dark brown and when I looked in the mirror the whites of my eyes were that same brown color. That was really scary. Obviously, there was something wrong.

What to do? Twenty-five year-olds don't get sick and of course they don't have a doctor. Do I go to a local emergency room and wait for help among all those bloody and broken? If so, which hospital? I could think of only one solution. I called my mother. I asked her to make an appointment for me with our family physician. Then I packed a bag, just in case it really was serious, and got on the subway, brown eyes and all, and traveled to Brooklyn. Dr. Hantman took one look at me and said, "Alan, you have hepatitis."

Hepatitis is caused by a virus infection. The Internet tells us it is most commonly transmitted by dirty conditions or by consuming contaminated food or water.

"Today hepatitis A usually doesn't require treatment because it's a short-term illness. Bed rest may be recommended if symptoms cause a great deal of discomfort."

But this was sixty years ago and Dr. Hantman sent me directly to a local hospital where I remained for almost a week until my infection disappeared. Then he suggested I take another week off until I regained my strength.

That wasn't going to happen if I returned to the "City" and I certainly didn't want to spend a week listening to my mother's "I told you so's."

In desperation I telephoned my mother's sister, and my favorite aunt, Sadie, in Palm Beach. I explained the situation and asked if she could put me up for a week or so. Sadie's current husband, Joseph was an MD—an ears, nose and throat specialist. I figured if something went wrong, he would be able to steer me in the right direction.

For the next ten days, I rested and relaxed away from the tumult and craziness in New York. More importantly I had the opportunity to exchange family gossip with my aunt and the opportunity to learn the real stories behind my mother's family's total wackiness. For instance, I was dying to know about her husband's brother Ben, a pharmacist, who recently had been the lead story in New York City's tabloid newspapers. He was on trial for murdering his wife with poison and was acquitted. My mother's family knew he had gotten away with murder. After all, they explained, who knows more about poison than a pharmacist?

The moral of this story, my children, is, no matter your age remember the Boy Scout motto—"Be Prepared." Among the first things to do in a new neighborhood is to make a connection with a doctor who will serve you when the unexpected happens. And believe me it will. Also it's a good idea to scope out the hospitals in your area.

There is a postscript to these events. While recuperating in the hospital and at my aunt's house, I didn't shave. By the time I returned to work at the Ted Bates advertising agency, I had a full beard. I was quite proud of that beard. It gave me a Mephisthophelean look. I did notice however, that I may have been the only person in the agency sporting facial hair. I soon learned why.

Jim Kavanaugh, an account executive I worked with, and who

was my mentor, took me aside and scolded me. He said beards were taboo at the Bates Agency! "If you don't want to ruin your career, I suggest you go home or to a barbershop right now and shave." I did.

Can you imagine an advertising agency today where facial hair is taboo?

ART AND THE SLOAN FAMILY

When I entered junior high school I was introduced to classical music. Until December 26, 1959, the day I married Sally, I had almost no contact with art. Not in high school, not in college and certainly not as a bachelor in New York City. But there I was age twenty-seven, marrying a professional artist with a degree in art history from Brown University that included a second major at the Rhode Island School of Design.

From that day forward, I have been surrounded by art, immersed in art and I live in a family focused on art. Doug, my oldest, a feature writer and a television show-runner, is a rock musician and has extraordinary artistic skills. He is an automobile "afficianado" and his portraits of autos compare most favorably to those by famous designers you see in magazines.

Julia, the middle child, like her mother is a professional artist. She has a Masters in Fine Art from Columbia University and teaches in the STEAM program that introduces art to school children of all ages. As an artist, she has created her own niche. Her paintings portray an environment in which humans and animals live together in an imaginary realm. She has shown in numerous exhibitions and her work is in demand. If you'd like to view her paintings go to juliamarchand.com.

Alix, our youngest, is an art entrepreneur. At one time she owned a major gallery in New York City but closed that space to return to the West Coast. She now represents a stable of artists whom she exhibits in "pop-up" galleries nationwide. Alix teaches a college course for fledging artists on the business of art and has written the accompanying text book entitled *Launching Your Art Career*.

She has written and published a mystery novel, entitled *Pet Sitter* (available on Amazon) and is currently working on the sequel.

Inspiring us all is my wife, Sally. Sally is an accomplished artist who has participated in countless exhibitions and been awarded numerous prizes. Her work is in the collections of many admirers. She is still painting today in her studio here at MPTF and she is in the process of organizing a series of workshops for MPTF residents. You can see some of her recent work on the internet at SallySloan. com.

With Sally's help and her encyclopedic knowledge of art history, I have gone from a twenty-seven-year-old neophyte to someone who not only enjoys the visual arts but has made art a basic part of my life. In fact, when we lived in Sarasota, Florida, I was chairman of the board of the Art Center and helped curate a number of art exhibitions. Sally will tell you that when she needs an outside eye to aid in solving a problem with a painting, she often asks me for advice.

Together we have visited art and architecture, modern and traditional, all over the world. Wherever we traveled, we purchased local art and we even raised our family in a work of art—a home designed by celebrated architect Richard Neutra. I have no favorite work of art except for the piece by Sally hanging in the Museum of Art in Kamchatka, Russia. There are however works of art that remain with me still—for example the stained-glass windows of St. Chapelle in Paris, the stone carving of the Annunciation above the doorway of a church in Vienna and the Xian tomb terracotta soldiers.

Despite my sixty-year connection to art, I still can't draw a straight line.

MY FIRST CHRISTMAS

Religion was never an important part of my life. We attended synagogue occasionally on the high holy days but I had no strong connection to either the Jewish faith or to religions in general. I did sing the obligatory Christmas carols in school but I had no idea what they meant. I can remember one time growing up, I was probably ten or eleven, when one of my young neighborhood friends, who I had fouled during a basketball game, accused me of killing Christ. I didn't know what he was talking about. I shrugged it off. The game continued without incident and I never followed up on his accusation.

Sally and I were married on December 26th, 1959. One year later we were driving to Lincoln, Massachusetts, where at the the age of twenty-eight, I was about to celebrate my first Christmas.

Lincoln is a suburb northwest of Boston. Many years ago it was a part of Concord and has the same charm as that Colonial icon. Many of the houses in Lincoln date back to revolutionary war days. Christmas dinner would be taking place in Sally's grandfather's house—originally a hut on the main road to Boston during the French and Indian War and expanded into an inn prior to the War of 1812. Robert Douglas Donaldson arrived in Concord in the 1890s after emigrating from Scotland to Newfoundland. He was an apprentice carpenter and had written a letter to a relative in Somerville, Massachusetts, inquiring whether there "was an opportunity for a hard working honest young man." Obviously there was, because by the 1920s he had become one of the most important builder/contractors in the Boston area.

He built hospitals, university buildings, the Lincoln Town Hall and hundreds of homes in the area. Today, Donaldson homes—many of them more than one hundred years old—are prized for their construction and sell for premium rates in the Boston area.

Robert Donaldson was also a successful family builder. He had four sons and two daughters. He saw to it that each one of them attended, and graduated from either Harvard or Wellesley. All six established themselves in excellent careers in their chosen fields. And all six maintained close personal relationships with one another for the rest of their lives. They were the definition of the word *family*.

There were thirteen grandchildren in all and my Sally was the oldest of that next generation. A total of forty-one family members would be attending Christmas dinner along with some foreign student friends of the current crop of college attendees.

I had been in Lincoln several times since we were married and had met many in Sally's family but never all at the same time with the entire group of relatives. Sally had briefed me on what to expect but nevertheless, I had the same feeling as Daniel must have had entering the lion's den. We arrived in Lincoln on Christmas eve and spent the evening at Sally's parents' house.

The next morning, we had a leisurely breakfast and then exchanged gifts under Sally's parents' tree. In the late morning Sally's mother left to join the other women in the family who would be preparing Christmas Dinner. At about 2:00 p.m., Bob and I, along with the rest of the Donaldson Clan, joined them at the Big House. In the dining room was a wonderfully decorated table for the adults and a similarly decorated table in an adjoining room for the children who were not yet ready to sit with the adults. There was a ceiling-high Christmas tree loaded with ornaments, lights, icicles and the like under which each family had placed one gift for all of the other families. Sally's father, Bob, usually hand-fashioned his family's gift. One year I remember he made wire and brass fireplace screens—probably spending months to complete what must have been a Herculean task.

I looked around in amazement. This was a *Saturday Evening Post* cover—a scene right out of a Norman Rockwell illustration. I was mesmerized and was having trouble relating this to Christmas and the lifetime of stories that had been part of my Jewish experience. Where were the crosses and crucifixes? Where was Jesus? Soon cocktails and wine were available and as I mixed with my in-laws and basked in their welcoming conversation I began to understand that I had been accepted as a member of this extraordinary family. Then dinner was served—a lavish feast with all the courses associated with Christmas dining including roast turkeys, stuffing, mashed potatoes, and gravy. That was accompanied by creamed onions, mashed sweet potatoes and mashed turnips with lots of butter. For dessert, the family had ordered Christmas fantasies—ice cream confections shaped like all types of festive Christmas decorations.

After dinner there was a traditional ritual to be followed. The men collected the dishes and washed and dried them laughing and joking all the while.

There was a wooden board nailed to the wall next to the cabinet over the sink. This year's dishwasher signed his name so that there would be no questions next year as to whose turn it was. Then the men gathered together outside for the annual touch football game. I thought to myself shades of the Kennedys, but this game was not about winning and losing as much as making room for the supper that the women were putting together inside. I was twenty-eight and still able to play, so I survived the two-hour marathon game without a major mistake and my reputation as an athlete still intact.

At about 5:00 p.m., we went inside for a sit-down supper. Cocktails again and a full New England dinner consisting of a baked ham, baked beans, all kinds of salads and vegetables, and another dessert festival with homemade pies, and everyone's favorite—Aunt Jean's sponge cake. After supper we trudged back to Sally's parents' house, hopefully never to eat again. I had made it through the day on my best behavior and without a faux pas, connecting with my new relatives and looking forward to returning for the next Lincoln family event the July Fourth parade.

The next day we returned to New York City. As I drove I tried to compare my own family's only holiday event, Passover, with what I had just been a part of. Our Seder, with approximately thirty in attendance, took place in a large private room over my aunt and uncle Rapoports' Second Avenue restaurant. The evening was steeped in religion with my grandfather, aged ninety plus, reciting prayers occasionally joined by some of the men in my family of my mother's generation. Most of the conversation was a hostile competitive battle in which each of my aunts tried to outdo the other. My mother, who had married young, against the advice of her sisters, was usually taken to task while my father and I were forced to listen to the invective. It was a no-fun affair, mean and spiteful, in contrast to the affection and camaraderie I had just been a part of.

For the first time I had learned what it meant to be a member of an extended family. My first Christmas taught me to treasure that experience and I vowed that my children would always have that sense of family. Sally was three months pregnant that Christmas. She was the oldest child in her generation and our child would be the first in the Donaldson family's next generation. Parenthetically, I always suspected that Sally's announcement of our forthcoming child that Christmas had made my entry into her family a whole lot easier.

One final note and it's a note about finality. Sally and I have yet to decide on a final place for our ashes. I would like them to be buried in the Donaldson family plot in Lincoln. I believe that might be an incentive for my children to visit Lincoln and in doing so remain in contact with their extended family. Also I would like to be buried with what has become my extended family. Finally, it's a very picturesque cemetery, part of American history dating back many generations and as a scholar of American politics and history I would like to have that as my final resting place.

Sally, in contrast, would like her ashes buried here in the Los Angeles area. She doesn't think our children or grandchildren, after the initial interment would ever find the time to visit Lincoln and, in fact, many of the most recent generation of Donaldsons have left Lincoln and are living all over the US. In truth, I believe she makes a good point. However, while writing this chapter, I believe I may have come up with a solution acceptable to both of us. Why don't we bury our ashes in both places? Each plot would have half our ashes beneath one headstone and if space was at a premium, our ashes could be mixed together in one urn. Romantic as well as practical! How's that for a solution, Sally?

NUGGETS

Nuggets could have been a Damon Runyon character. His real name was Morris Klompus and sometimes we called him Billy Bogash Shit-ass Shamash. I have no idea why!

We first met on the basketball courts in Coney Island. We weren't friends, but we played with and against each other and occasionally talked while waiting for our "Next."

Nuggets didn't look like a basketball player, he was about 5'10" and on the heavy side but he was smart and had "game." I considered myself a player and I was on the court most days—rain or shine.

I was attending the Baruch Business School at City College and Nuggets, then a senior at Lincoln High, would be going to City next year along with other Coney Islanders—Murray Selinger, commonly known as "the Pu," and Joe Gootter—his nickname, "The Gootch"— his slogan, "You may be good, but he's Gootter."

Little did I realize that Nuggets would soon become a major personality at the college. New York City during that era was the unquestioned capital of college basketball in the US. City College had an excellent team, nationally ranked along with crosstown rivals St. John's and LIU. On Tuesday mornings during basketball season, Nuggets, usually dressed in a leopard-skin patterned shirt and occasionally wearing a tie picturing a young boy peeing, would be passing out the weekly basketball pool sheets to the entire student body.

Later in the week, he would collect our completed cards along with our wagers and cash. There was no way Nuggets could have financed that effort—hundreds of students were participating—but he wouldn't tell us if he was working for a bookmaker or directly for organized crime.

City College became the only team ever to win both the NCAA and NIT tournament championships in the same year. Nuggets, because of his sports card business, was fast becoming a school legend. But it all came to an abrupt end in 1951. The Cinderella City College squad, that was favored to repeat as champions and was being touted as the team to represent the US in the 1952 Olympics, had lost seven games—almost half its schedule—by mid-February.

Obviously something was amiss, and on early Sunday morning February 18, we learned what. At a house plan event, the party came to a screeching halt when a radio bulletin interrupted our music program to report that three of the CCNY stars had been arrested for point shaving. We were stunned! I asked Nuggets if he had known what was going on, but he claimed innocence and I sort of believed him.

That was the end of the basketball program at City College and at a number of other major universities as well. More than thirty athletes nationwide were arrested. It was, in fact, the end of New York City's reign as America's basketball mecca and it was the end of Nuggets' basketball card effort. Parenthetically, he did distribute football cards the following season, but City had no football team and there really wasn't much interest in the sport.

In 1951, my family moved from Coney Island to the City Line section of Brooklyn and, although I continued to see Nuggets on campus and at parties, we were never as close as in those early days when we played ball on the playground. In the ensuing years after graduation, I saw him three or four times at most.

Unhappily, that's not the end of the story. From mutual friends, I learned that Nuggets was married and had a son. The word was she was a real catch. A surprise to many of us because Nuggets' former behavior was at best bizarre. Furthermore he didn't have much going for him in the "looks" department. He was considerably overweight and was significantly fashion impaired. I had also heard that Nuggets had gone straight—he was employed by the government as a counselor/social worker and was supplementing his income as a part-time accountant.

However, the word was that Nuggets still was hanging around with some very shady friends.

One day, in 1974, one of those friends asked Nuggets if he would accompany him on a trip to Boston. He wanted some company on the long trip from Brooklyn. The friend was in the sports pennant business and he was going to Boston to open up a new territory. Unbeknownst to Nuggets, and perhaps to his friend—although I doubt that—sports pennants in Boston was a mob business. While the friend was doing business all Nuggets had to do was wait for him in the car.

Several days later, Morris Klompus, alias Nuggets, age forty-two, and his friend were found dead in the trunk of that car in the vicinity of Logan Airport. They had been executed mob-style and the murders have never been solved.

CONEY ISLAND

I had just graduated high school when we moved to Coney Island. *The* Coney Island. In those days, our family moved often and usually I was upset when we moved. I never did figure out why, but it seemed like every year or two we moved. I suspect it had something to do originally with the Depression and later on with World War II. Moving meant a new neighborhood, a new school, and new friends. And then, just as were settled in, we would move again.

The previous two summers, we had rented a bungalow just two blocks from the beach. That bungalow was difficult to rent in the winter and so my parents were able to make a year-round deal that was beneficial to both landlord and the tenant—us. It meant that we would probably be there for a while.

A new neighborhood school would not be an issue. I was starting college and that was at the CCNY downtown campus in Manhattan on the corner of 23rd Street and Lexington Avenue.

As for neighborhood friends, because we had summered in Coney Island the past two years, I had already made those connections. There were two kids my age on my street that I knew pretty well and I had gotten to know several other kids playing basketball in the park. Also, there was a private teen boys club I hoped to join.

I can hear you saying to yourself, "Coney Island is an amusement park. Do people really live there?" Yes, on both counts. But first it's important to understand the geography. Originally, Coney Island was an island off the southernmost tip of the borough of Brooklyn in New York City. In the late 1800s, part of the gap was filled in and the island was connected to the mainland. When I lived there, the Island consisted of four distinct neighborhoods.

On the extreme western end was Sea Gate—a small, four- or five-blocks wide, upscale, gated enclave. Moving east was the section called Coney Island, which stretched from 37th Street in the west to15th Street and included a thriving community of 30,000 plus residents. From there to 1st Street was the amusement park area—still part of Coney Island and bordered by Brighton Beach. Finally, at the eastern end of the island, Manhattan Beach, another very exclusive area, was located.

The last stop in Brooklyn on the BMT subway line was Coney Island. When you got off the train, you were on Stilwell Avenue. Several blocks straight ahead were the boardwalk, the beach, and the bay. If you turned left, that's east, off Stilwell you entered the amusement area—Luna Park, the Cyclone roller coaster, hundreds of game parlors, scores of eateries, and best of all, Nathan's Famous Hot Dogs at 13th Street and Surf Avenue. More on Nathan's later.

If you boarded a connecting bus and went west, you entered the Coney Island residential section, about five blocks wide and about twenty blocks long and consisting primarily of bungalows and two-story connected row houses. We lived on 25th Street, two blocks from the beach. The beach was spectacular—at least a block wide and never overly crowded, even in the height of the summer season. Although hundreds of thousands of New Yorkers invaded the beach every summer day, at 25th Street we were just far enough away from the amusement park area to discourage visitors. Also on the Boardwalk, which stretches from one end of the island to the other, almost all the shops and restaurants were clustered in the amusement park area.

My first year in Coney Island, I was able to join a social club. It was a group of about fifteen neighborhood teenage boys, ages sixteen to eighteen, who chipped in to pay the rent on a basement apartment. The apartment was sparsely furnished with several used sofas and chairs, a few lamps and a record player. We hung out, had occasional parties and on weekends in the late evening, we gathered to exchange stories, most of them stories about our romantic conquests.

Seventy years later, I still remember Heshie Siegel, at midnight Saturday, bursting through the door shouting, "Boy, did I get her hot."

Most large groups will eventually break up into smaller cliques and this club was no exception. About six months after I joined, one of the guys in my clique learned that the Amron Club was dissolving. They were in their twenties, had been together for years, and now many of them had outgrown the club mentality. The Amrons were notorious in Coney Island both for their amorous adventures and for their club house. Amron spelled backward was the name of the first girl, Norma, who had lost her virtue in their lavishly appointed headquarters.

In contrast to our dingy basement hangout, the Amrons had rented a storefront on 36th Street and converted it into an eye-appealing and welcoming environment. Unlike our basement hideout, the girls they dated were impressed and felt comfortable in the club. The furniture was almost new, there was indirect lighting throughout and the sound system was strategically placed, with the finest speakers in numerous locations. It was a veritable "Honey Trap."

It was an expensive proposition, but by merging with another group who we knew were looking for a club house, we were able to make it work. Of course we kept the Amron name. In only six months I had been transformed from a newly arrived unknown quantity to an Amron. Believe me, socially that was a big deal in Coney Island and I was determined to take advantage of it.

Unfortunately my college career was in major trouble.

JULIA

Sally and I have differing views of our daughter Julia's teen and post-teen years. She describes them as restless and adventuresome. I call them bizarre.

There were some minor happenings early on, but the so-called "restlessness" truly began during her senior year in high school.

One morning we received a call from the Calabasas High School principal asking us to come in and meet with her about our daughter, Julia. We learned that unbeknownst to us Julia had not been attending school her final semester. She had intercepted her report card, as well as all other notices from school. Julia confessed that she and her friends had spent their school days at the beach. As a result she did not graduate with her class, could not enter a four-year college, spent the summer in school repeating her senior semester and in the fall, enrolled in a community college in San Luis Obispo.

Two years later, upon graduation, Sally and Julia made the tour of East Coast colleges and universities. On their visit to American University in Washington, D.C., they arrived in the midst of a raucous student demonstration. She immediately decided that American U. would be the place for her. There she became good buddies with Dan Mathews and that led to another string of what I would describe as mind-boggling events.

After graduation, Julia returned to Los Angeles where she worked in odd jobs while she pursued her ambition to become a fine art photographer.

Dan Matthews joined PETA, People for the Ethical Treatment of Animals, and after several years became its director. In that role, Dan traveled the world creating incidents that brought attention to the PETA cause. On numerous occasions, he called on his old friend Julia to join him. Julia was a drop-dead gorgeous blonde who was a skilled communicator and could be available on almost no notice. Dan was openly gay which meant they could save significant dollars by bunking together wherever they went.

We really didn't understand what was involved until the afternoon my old friend Kive called and asked if I had been watching CNN. I tuned in and there, in a brief segment, were Julia, Dan and several Japanese PETA members marching down the Ginza in Tokyo, apparently "buck-naked" holding a sign in front of them proclaiming, in Japanese, "I'd rather be naked than wear fur." They were protesting against the International Furriers Association who were holding their annual meeting in Tokyo. And as the afternoon progressed, and the telephone calls increased, what had been a brief segment turned into a feature story which was rebroadcast every hour. The following Sunday morning as Sally and I were peacefully enjoying our morning coffee, we received a telephone call. It was from our friend Evie asking if we had seen the *LA Times*. There in the magazine section was a full-page story with accompanying photo depicting Julia in all her naked splendor. Parenthetically, Julia to this day maintains she was wearing a body stocking—and Sally believes her.

That was just the first of many similar episodes. For instance there was the day when Sally heard on her car radio that Julia and Dan had been arrested in Singapore. Obviously we were worried—Singapore is noted for its less than hospitable jails. The next day we received a call from Julia reporting that they were in Singapore to promote the vegan life style and had not received the necessary permits. Their stay behind bars was brief and after their release they held a press conference at which Julia complimented the prison staff for their excellent vegan meal. She was very proud because that line became the tag for the subsequent worldwide press coverage.

Moving on to Moscow, Dan and Julia had been unable to make the usual preparations for this trip—it was during the time of great unrest in the Soviet Union soon after the Berlin Wall had been breached. Their plan was to spread the vegetarian gospel by serving veggie burgers in front of the McDonald's in Red Square. This time not only did they not have permits, but they had been unable to find facilities to prepare the burgers and buns they were taking with them. On the plane Julia explained their plight to a fellow passenger, a Russian, who offered his kitchen. That solved one problem and they decided to forge ahead. Two days later they set up a table in the square wearing T-shirts in Cyrillic with the slogan, "Trotsky was a vegetarian." Not too smart, considering that Trotsky had been assassinated in Mexico by the NKVD. Their luck held. The soldiers supposedly policing the square had passed out. Too much vodka! Unmolested, they were able to attract a large curious crowd and once again made international news.

There was also the time that they dressed in a cow costume—Julia was the rear end—and danced in the streets of Rio at the International Climate Change convention denouncing the meat industry for the methane cows were contributing to the atmosphere.

In retrospect, I would agree that Julia was restless and adventuresome and her actions were somewhat bizarre particularly for someone who was neither a vegetarian nor a vegan.

In attempting to understand her behavior, we've come up with three possible explanations. Any one of which seems to make sense. Perhaps it's genetic.

Sally's mother, Dorothy Lloyd, was a true adventuress. In 1924, upon graduating from Oberlin College, she applied for a teaching position at the American School in the Peking, China, suburbs. Remember, this was during the Chinese Revolution, a particularly violent and blood-thirsty period when the opposing warlords would place the severed heads of their enemies on pikes in the streets near to the school. She returned home after three years via the Siberian railroad across China, Manchuria, and Europe and then by ship to the United States.

Then there's the possibility it has something to do with the environment of her early childhood. This may be a stretch, but sometimes we credit Julia's behavior to the fact that when she was just a year old we moved to Lima, Peru. Spanish was the language of her nursemaids and her first language. After a year, we returned to the US and there were numerous times when Julia could not make family members and friends understand what she was saying. Perhaps her subsequent behavior was a function of that confusion.

Finally, our third explanation is "middle-child syndrome." Julia is three years younger than her brother Douglas and three years older than her sister Alexandra.

"Middle-child syndrome" is defined by psychiatrists as the feeling of exclusion by middle children. This effect occurs because the first child is more prone to receiving privileges and responsibilities (by virtue of being the oldest), while the youngest in the family is more likely to receive indulgences.

I'm partial to this theory because my sister Sandie is a middle child and displays some of the same idiosyncrasies as Julia. And also because a number of social scientific studies have concluded that:

"Although middles are neglected by parents, they actually benefit from this in the long run. They become more independent, think outside the box, feel less pressure to conform, and are more empathetic."

And that certainly describes our Julia.

P. S. Today Julia, age fifty-four, has a master of fine arts and teaches art in the Oakland, California, school system. She is also a very successful artist. To view her work go to juliamarchand.com, and she is the mother of two very well-adjusted children. Notice I said *two*, not three. 🖋

Longing is difficult to write about. It is the search for something that isn't there. Where did it go? Was it taken? Did I give it away? Was it ever here?

JOHN DEL REGNO

EXCERPTS FROM "A BUMS LIFE"

I have decided to write about my thirty-eight years as an actor. Back and forth between feast and famine, going from nowhere to the verge of celebrity and financial security, to defeat and back again, this is my story.

For most of the world, people have to make a living to eat, to have a roof over their head. Most work at jobs they would quit in a minute if they hit the lottery or inherited a large amount of money. There are a lucky few that earn a living at something they love, that they would do for free. Can anything be better than that? I don't think so. To look forward to go to work, free of depressing Sundays because tomorrow is Monday and back to that crappy job.

That's what I wanted, not money or fame, although that would be a nice fringe benefit, I wanted freedom. So, after chasing my tail and going nowhere for the first thirty years of my life, I set out to be a professional actor. While I am not a household name, I am often recognized in a store or somewhere in public and strangers, sure they have met me before, would ask me if I was a chef in some restaurant or a cop that gave them a ticket.

I grew up in a tough working-class neighborhood on the lower east side of New York City. This was not the Manhattan of now, over-run by yuppies and wannabes from all over the world. This was the New York of the fifties and sixties, a concrete jungle of overcrowded slums. In those days, if you wanted to breathe some fresh air or to see a tree or ground that was not covered in asphalt or concrete you had to go uptown to Central Park, where you could get in trouble with uptown tough guys. It was the beginning of the post–World War II generation later called the baby boomers. Hordes of kids roaming the streets, fighting and playing street games with each other. Street games now all but extinct like stickball that used a hard rubber ball that would take off like a rocket when hit with an old broom handle. We would play in the street avoiding cars and open cellar doors. There was also touch football, handball, Johnny-on-the-Pony, Bottoms Up, and pitching quarters against a wall .The younger girls practiced all the latest dance steps like the Lindy, Cha Cha, The Slop, and the Twist.

In those days, if you wanted to play outside with the other kids, you had to be at least a competent street fighter, otherwise you would get your ass kicked every day for your lunch money, your belt, or whatever the tougher kids wanted from you. If you couldn't or wouldn't fight, you stayed home and helped your mother with housework. The only outlets were sports or crime. Drugs were not widespread then as either you were a hard-core junkie or not. There was no distinction between pot and heroin—if you did one, you did the other. If you were able to survive childhood, you were expected to do some kind of military service because being an able-bodied male, you had to serve the nation.

In my early tears, I had hoped my ticket out of poverty would be sports. I had speed, power, and determination but alas, my height stopped at 5 foot and 7 inches which meant that as my competition grew to 6 feet and more, no college would give me a scholarship which was the only way I could go on to higher education as there was no money in my family to send me. So, soon after graduating from high school I joined the US Navy. Why I did that, I am not sure. I could have gone to college. I was accepted, but I would have to work during the day and go to school at night. I guess at the time I needed to get away and military service was hanging over my head anyway in the form of the draft. So, I went away to the Navy for four years chasing Soviet Union submarines all over the world

After my four-year hitch was up, I got out of the Navy at twenty-three years old in 1968. Adjusting back to civilian life after the military can be difficult transition at any time. I entered smack in the middle of the hippie counter culture revolution. As I was away, I didn't experience the gradual change, so it was a shock to see the widespread drug use and what I thought at the time, unpatriotic attitudes toward their own country. But I was determined to begin my life after the Navy interruption, get a good paying job, find a good wife, and settle down with a family

It was hard to get close to these groovy, hippie women because I had nothing to talk about with them. I soon discovered, if you wanted to turn them off right away, tell them you were in the military. The immediate reaction was disgust and what an asshole you must be. So, the last four years of my life had to be a secret, otherwise I would be spending lonely Saturday nights with some of the other vets that were having a tough time, getting drunk and talking about the military. Looking back, I am glad I did it. I talk to friends of mine now that didn't serve and I feel that they regret not doing what men have been doing for thousands of years, protecting their homes and family. As women have the responsibility to bear children, a man's responsibility is to protect them.

I was trained as an aviation electrician in the navy and thought I could get a good job with the airlines. I applied but they said I would have to go back to school and get a degree to qualify for the position I sought. My competition in the job market were either eighteen-year-old recent high school graduates or at my age with a college degree. I could not wait to begin my life for another four years, so I took a job with Prudential Life Insurance as a sales agent. I hated it, but I got married to a girl I met in a bar and needed to have a good paying job. She came from a very pampered background and me being socially backward—I blame the Navy—made for an explosive combination. One year later, we were divorced. It took me a while to recover from this failure. I was the first person in my extended family to get a divorce.

A couple of years after the divorce, I recovered sufficiently to be dating a beautiful Latin girl I met on the subway. She was usually on the car that I entered and after we flirted a few times, I asked her out. We were both from different backgrounds but the subway threw us together and we fell in love. Her name was Doris and she didn't want to get married as she felt she was too young and coming from a large family, didn't want kids until she was at least twenty-five. I loved her so I would wait.

One day at the sales office, I was talking to a co-worker, Aaron Kollar, about how much we hated the job. He said I should be an actor as I was able to make people laugh and I could tell a good story. I said, "What do you do, fill out an application like any other job?"

He said, "Go to acting school and let the GI bill pay for it."

Something clicked inside my head—go to school and become an actor and let the government pay for it. It sounded logical. I always thought I could act if given the chance. As an only child, I developed a vivid imagination and I was a very good mimic.

It was 1973 and I had been out of the Navy for five years and in a rut. Who knows if Doris will ever marry me and I hated the sales job, I was ready for something new in my life. Aaron and I looked in the Yellow Pages for an acting school that was VA-approved. We found one and I signed up and paid tuition to a place called The New York Academy of Theatrical Arts in lower Manhattan.

I went to the office to sign up and this woman that I had to see, was sitting behind a desk with paper and books piled three feet high. What a mess, I thought, how could she find anything in that heap? This did not instill much confidence in me for the quality of the school but I filled out the application and paid for the first three months.

Even though I would be reimbursed by the VA, I felt I had done a stupid thing. After all, I was pushing thirty years old and should be thinking about my future, instead of wasting my VA grant on such an irresponsible venture.

My first class came around and I was not sure I would go. I was thinking, I had my own one-bedroom apartment in Astoria, Queens, I was driving a new Oldsmobile 442, and I was making pretty good money. Screw it. I'll drop the whole idea, who needs the headache? The few friends I told about this laughed, "Going to acting school learning to be poor," or "Yeah, right, another one of your crazy whims." I complained to Doris about the pain in the ass traveling downtown in the evening in Manhattan where the school was. She thought the idea of me going to acting school was great and she bragged to her friends, "my boyfriend, the actor." She said, "Go for the hell of it." She later regretted encouraging me to go when she found out the school was noted for teaching acting basics to models. So, I thought, the money was already paid, it turns Doris on, what the heck, I'll check it out.

I went a little early and just sat in my car there watching the entrance. A few people were milling around outside, and one thing became apparent, the caliber of women hanging outside the entrance to the school were usually out of my league. I had always been a night owl. Until now, if I saw one of these tall, beautiful, model looking women, I could appreciate them, but I wouldn't waste time and money buying them drinks because these beauties were usually looking for high rollers.

I waited in my car until the last minute and almost turned around to go back to Queens. I had to call upon every ounce of courage and walk into to this new world. When I got to the entrance, another woman was walking in with me and she said, "Hi," and I said, "Hi" back. She said it was her first time there and was nervous. I reassured her that it would be all right, besides, what can they do to you?

In the class, I sat in the back and just observed. Picking up on conversations before the class started, I observed that most had some kind of theatrical training either from college or community theater. When class started, the teacher asked each individual to stand up and state who they were and what acting they had done in the past. I dreaded my turn, I didn't want to tell the class, that not only had I never done a play, I had never even seen one. When it was my turn, I just said, I don't have much experience, but I am glad to be here.

I stayed with this school and had the time of my life. I learned about making noises like a cow and other animals. As no one in the class was a professional, I did not feel inadequate. On the contrary, I discovered that I liked it on stage and looked forward to bringing in scenes and monologues for the class. The class put a strain on my relationship with Doris. Previously she had not been jealous of other women, always confidant that no women could compete with her for me. Sometimes coming out of class, Doris would be waiting for me to see if I was talking to any of the women. This was embarrassing to me, but the aspiring actresses thought it was sexy. I tried to reassure Doris that I was all business, and I was.

One day, an instructor mentioned to a couple of us that we should audition for plays around town. "How?" I asked. He said to make up a resume of plays that you did scenes from and put down you did them in some obscure theater, pick up the trade papers, back-stage and show business, look for open calls that are casting your type and go for it. New York in those days had many non-union theaters so, why not? I picked out a couple of auditions, dressed in my Saturday-night clothes, packing my professional headshots and fake resume and went into the city for my first audition. My fate was sealed.

The day came around for my first audition in show business, I was already twenty-eight years old. At that age, a lot of actors were living large and already had a career, but so what, they don't know what I know. I was going to audition for a revival of *Feiffer's People*, a comedy by a well-known cartoonist, Jules Feiffer.

The show had already been running awhile and this audition was for replacements. The *Backstage* casting notice for the play listed several characters that I thought I may be right for, so I went.

I got there early and there were already about ten people waiting in the lobby of the theater, which was above a bar on Lexington Avenue. They were all sitting and studying a few pages in their hand. I looked around and I must have looked bewildered because this young actress, Theresa—who by the way was already an experienced actress at eighteen years old—asked me if I had signed in yet. I said, "No, where do you do that?"

She pointed to a desk and told me to pick up the sides.

"Then what?" I asked and she took me by the hand and helped me through the routine.

I looked over the material and it seemed pretty simple and straightforward, a guy trying to pick up a girl in a bar. After about an hour, I was called into audition for the director. I had played a lot of baseball in my time and the feeling of nervousness and focus getting up to bat was similar to going in to audition.

I went into the room and there were just two people—the director, a young guy, and a women who read the scene with me. When I read, the director laughed so hard he almost fell out of his chair. This was not a polite laugh or forced, this was something that came deep from his gut, by someone who was totally surprised by what he saw. When I walked out of the room, I felt like I was high, Theresa, who had already auditioned was gone. Because it was in the middle of the day, I took the subway there but I was so full of energy I walked over the 59th Street Bridge all the way home.

When I finally got home and checked for messages, there was a message from the stage manager giving me an appointment for a callback. When I told some of my classmates at the school that I went on an audition and have a callback, their reaction was mixed and I did detect some jealousy.

When I mentioned it to Doris, I thought I saw pain in her big, beautiful brown eyes. I wanted to comfort her. I felt if I asked her to marry me right then, in her moment of weakness she would have said yes. But then I thought, as I was holding her in my arms and telling her not to worry, she would want me to give up this crazy idea about acting because she wouldn't go down that road with me. So, I gave up an opportunity to be happy with this beautiful woman and have a family. Instead, I chose to chase a dream.

I went to the callback and recognized some of the actors from the audition, including Theresa. She nodded her head hello to me, so I walked over to where Theresa and some others were talking. They all sounded so optimistic, talking about their auditions for commercials and how some agent said he would work for them. I stood there silently so they wouldn't know how green I was.

The acting class I was taking consisted mainly of people working 9-to-5 jobs and who had not taken the plunge, like myself. But here I was in the company of actors pursuing acting full time and some actually making money at it occasionally. I felt accepted because after all, I was at a callback.

When it was my turn to audition, I walked into a room with six people sitting behind a large desk. I felt their eyes burning a hole through me. I made what I thought were the same acting choices I made for the first audition but this time nobody fell out of their chairs. When I came to a line that I thought would get a big laugh, all I heard were a few snickers.

As I was walking out of the room, somewhat dejected that I didn't get the response I expected, one of the people that was in the room came out and asked me if I could sing. I lied and said yes. I have always had a mental block about singing in public ever since I was rejected for the choir when I was seven. He asked me to sing something for him and I said I couldn't remember any songs so he suggested "Happy Birthday." What was I to do? I couldn't say I didn't remember that song, so I belted out a few lines of "Happy Birthday" and the producer said thank you very much and walked away.

That evening I got a call that I was cast and given a rehearsal schedule. Maybe they couldn't get anyone else, after all the show had already been reviewed and was going to close in two weeks. BUT I GOT THE PART. ✐

For the rest of "A Bum's Life," please visit: http://abumslife-regno.blogspot. com.

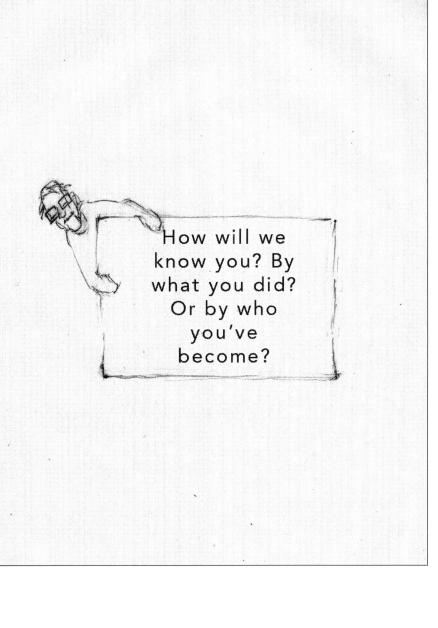

How will we know you? By what you did? Or by who you've become?

TONY LAWRENCE

THROUGH THE WINDOWPANE

i saw her through the windowpane
bright steps and sunshine hair
guiding with sure hand and foot
a carriage meant for royal prerogative

i thought for all the world right then
a princely child was being thrust
down pathways trimmed with lilac stems
where only ancient footsteps promenaded

but soon discovered I that she
held in that royal earthly pram
a tiny canine princely form
with wistful face and dignified three-footedness

the queen and silky scion
left my mind intrigued and touched
so captivated by their stately pace
that surely I knew then I had to see much more of them

and more of them did I see
in dining room with coffee cup in hand
offering myself as lonely men do
trying to gain her confidence
with stumbling and banal male platitudes

but fortunately she saw in me
something more than what I thought was there
and suddenly the world I knew
so completely turned around
my head now filled with glee and adoration

suddenly, like some old fool
panning for nuggets in a river bed
i'd struck it rich for luck or fate
had surely brought these precious jewels into my life
and now there was nothing sweeter than the taste of gratefulness

her sovereign name is Madeleine
how lovely is the sound of that
but Madi is the tag preferred and
it suits her vibrant energy
the way she moves through life with such wholeheartedness

what then can be left to say about Dexter?
rusty coat and beady little black eyes
that reach deep into your soul
that one leg in front sturdy as greasewood
and peeking from his royal stroller he gives new meaning to
melancholy

so what I saw through the windowpane
misted from my breath the world opaque
has now become a clear and present happiness
a family life that lifts my spirit and my heart
a love so deep and strong that nothing on this earth could alter it

To Madi and Dexter
From Tony with all my love

WINTER WOMAN

Long ago,
In some distant place
A narrow, deep inlet of the sea,
Between high cliffs,
In Norway or Iceland,
Formed by submergence of a glaciated valley,
A woman, carrying a firstborn inside her
Made her way searching for food.

Long ago,
When permafrost covered the naked ground
And bands of elk roamed great northern land
In forests verdant, and the fox scampered
And the bear slept beneath the white
Blanket, with only his breath
Noting his survival.

Long ago,
It was this lone winter woman
Seeking food and shelter to appease
Her own hunger and to save the child yet born,
Who sought out the red berries left from spring
And wisps of green rhizome that grows
Horizontally underground
With a stem that puts out lateral shoots,
Adventitious roots that peek at intervals.

Long ago,
It was this new ancestral heartbeat drum
This nascent child who came into existence,
Displaying signs of future potential from
Nothing more than hydrogen freshly
Generated in a reactive form, given a name
And crying out that she was here.

Long ago,
It was she who began the long line of
Forebears who sang of summers fierce
And winters cold, and begat the stream of
Evolutionary and genetic line of descent,
This ancestry of a rose so complex that would lead
Eventually to the perfect design
That is known to us as MADI.

To my wife, Madi
With all my love forever
Christmas 2017

UNDERSTANDING WHERE LOVE IS
TONY'S VOW TO MADI

At one time we were like
    Broken stars
Little more than quiet whispers—
    There are still spaces in
Our togetherness
    But when I look into your eyes
My heart near your heart
    I know that our love is strong
Like the fragrance of orchids
    The stars are fire now
And even when they grow older
    When there is sad or singing weather
Our tender looks will become habits
    We will be partners

My dearest Madi, I make this vow to you—

My heart will always be your shelter;
The life we have left
I will always try to make worthwhile for us both—
Our independence will always be equal;
Two souls but a single seed,
I will always trust you beyond words
And through pride, pleasure, tears, no matter what
We will be as one out of two
Each still a whole
Both understanding where love really is.
I will love you, Madi until my breath is gone—

In writing, humanity is our canvas, humility our medium, enlightenment our purpose.

MADI SMITH-LAWRENCE

"Once you have flown, you will walk the earth with your eyes turned skyward. For there you have been and there you long to be."
—Leonardo da Vinci

Though I have arrived at the age of seventy-nine, I always have and will continue to call my daddy, my Daddy. Whenever I refer to him, he is Daddy. No matter how old or sophisticated I think I may be, he is my Daddy.

My Daddy was a pilot. He joined the Army Air Corps at the age of fourteen, eating a bunch of bananas and drinking lots of water so he could pass the physical. His education was only to the sixth grade, but he was eager to learn and fearless. He was the only son of a family of thirteen girls born on June 7, 1902.

Daddy fought in the Nicaraguan Campaign, flew lighter than air, worked on the Spirit of St. Louis, was dear friends of Howard Hawks, Will Rogers, and Wiley Post. Amelia Earhart and Pancho Barnes were his hanger mates.

In his later years, I would drive up to Lancaster to visit Daddy at his convalescent home. His favorite outing was to have breakfast at Denny's. Old habits are hard to change. He would reminisce of bygone days and though Daddy was a quiet man, when he spoke of flying his eyes would brighten and you could see the years vanish from his face. I asked him if there was anything he hadn't flown. He said he would have liked to have flown in a glider plane. Though he had piloted everything from a lighter than air to jet, he longed for the quiet ecstasy of soaring.

So when I got back to work on Monday, I researched glider planes for rent in the desert near my Daddy. Several weeks later, after

I checked out the experience of gliding with this pilot, a friend of mine drove me out for the big surprise.

After picking up Daddy, we arrived at the glider. The pilot approached Daddy. They sat and talked for a long time, while the pilot's eyes got bigger and bigger. My Daddy told him of his history and why he was thrilled to fly again.

I should have prefaced this sooner, to explain that my Daddy was not well. He could no longer walk, had had open heart surgery, Parkinson's disease etc., etc. He was eighty-six.

As we wheeled him to the plane and lifted him in the cockpit, my heart sank. I had so many mixed emotions. What if he had a heart attack while soaring, would he be okay, what if he died up there? My friend consoled me saying that if he died, he was doing what he loved. They were in the sky what seemed like hours and I held my breath for the entire time.

When they landed, I rushed to the glider and saw the biggest smile on Daddy's face, and his eyes were shining like I hadn't seen in a very long time. We lifted Daddy out of the plane and into his wheel-chair. The pilot shook Daddy's hand and thanked him for sharing his history. He said he was honored to have flown with him.

A few weeks later, my Daddy passed away. My friend helped me with the arrangements one must make, and then on his birthday we took my Daddy for his last flight. The pilot slid open his window, my friend read my Daddy's favorite poem as I released Daddy's ashes high above where his soul will fly forever.

Petar Sardelich

JOHN TOWEY

OUR MIRACLE BABY

When I turned thirty-six years old, I was hired as a guest actor at a summer theatre in Cortland, New York. I had the privilege of portraying Atticus Finch in a stage adaptation of Harper Lee's novel *To Kill a Mockingbird*. I had never been offered the role of a man with that much integrity, wisdom, compassion, nobility, and of course, parenting skills. I felt honored to have been chosen and tried to infuse into my portrayal as many of those qualities as I could. Living with that character that summer was the first time I'd ever felt like a real parent and I loved the feeling. Of course, I had no idea of the endless responsibilities that were entailed by becoming an actual parent.

Almost from the minute I stopped drinking and smoking weed, when I was thirty-eight years old, I had an overwhelming and unexplainable desire to have a child. The woman whom I eventually married, made it clear to me that she also wanted a child. We married in 1982, after we'd been lovers for nine years and now made the decision to start a family.

We tried everything—the perfect sexual position at the right time of the month to conceive. Eventually she began to take fertility drugs. After a year of this, we discovered that she was unable to conceive, so we put the word out to our relatives and friends that we were now open to adopt. It was a disheartening discovery to find out that the adoption agencies were unable to qualify us because of the unsteady nature of our profession and because of our ages; I was forty-three at the time and Henrietta was forty-eight. Having chosen acting as a career, we were both very used to rejection since it goes along with the nature of our profession; constantly auditioning and constantly looking for the next job, so we took this rejection from the adoption agencies in our stride.

Having both acted in separate productions at the Guthrie Theatre in previous years, we were both invited, independently, in the summer of 1984 to become two of twenty-seven members of a newly-formed acting company at the Guthrie. We were given a year's contract with wonderful roles for the entire season. We were thrilled. We stayed there for three years.

Early in the morning of April 1, 1986, while still living and working in Minneapolis, Henrietta received a fateful phone call. The man on the other end was a friend of the woman with whom she had attended college at Northwestern University thirty years earlier. The man said, "I understand you're interested in adopting a child." Henrietta said, "Yes, we are." "Well," he said, "a healthy baby boy was born to an underage girl in a hospital in Newark, New Jersey, last night and her mother wants to do a direct adoption. If you can arrive here within forty-eight hours with adoption papers that the girl and her mother will have to sign, you'll be given this baby boy."

Stunned, Henrietta hung up the phone and relayed the information to me. I said, without hesitation, "Yes, let's go."

We were to pick up the adoption papers at our lawyer's office in New York city and be back at the small hospital in Newark before 9:00 a.m. when the teenage mother was to be discharged. We took the earliest flight we could find directly to the Newark airport. We had friends staying in our New York apartment, so we rented a car at the airport and drove to Montclair, New Jersey, where Henrietta's nephew and family lived and who were more than happy to offer their third-floor bedroom to us for as long as we needed it. It was April 2, 1986. Just before falling asleep on the night before our drive to the hospital, Henrietta turned to me in bed and said, "We don't have to go through with this if you don't want to."

I said, "I want us to be dragged into the next century and this little boy is going to help us get there."

Early the next day we drove into New York City, picked up the adoption papers, drove back to Newark and were in the parking lot of the hospital before 9:00 a.m., ready to claim our baby boy. We were both very excited and at the same time terrified. I was now forty-six years old and Henrietta was fifty-one.

The parking lot at the hospital was empty when we arrived, except for one nurse who had been waiting for us. She embraced us both and told us to look up to the second-floor windows of the hospital where there were at least a dozen nurses waving to us. The transfer of the child could not be done within the hospital, so the mother of the girl, who was younger than either Henrietta or me, approached us. She signed the adoption papers on the hood of our car, then took them to her daughter, who was just getting into their car thirty yards away at the back entrance of the hospital. She signed the papers. A nurse then handed the young grandmother the baby. It was a cold morning and Henrietta had gotten back into our car. The grandmother approached me with the child warmly wrapped in a blanket with a bright mustard-colored wool cap snugly on his head. She gently transferred him to me and waited until Henrietta rolled down the window and I handed the boy in to her. Then the grandmother gave me an envelope.

We thanked her, said goodbye and watched her walk to her car. The nurses on the second floor all waved to us again as we pulled out of the parking lot and drove back to Montclair. The note in the envelope was written by the mother of the young girl.

Sitting in the passenger seat while holding our baby, Henrietta opened the envelope. The note was written in long-hand on lined paper. It read, "Dear New Parents: My daughter and her boyfriend did something very stupid. They are both excellent students and both on the honor roll at school. He plays football and is on the fencing team in his high school and is planning on attending college next year. They do not smoke or drink or do drugs of any kind. I wish you both a wonderful, happy life filled with love for this beautiful, precious child."

We drove the rest of the way to Montclair in silence, knowing this decision would completely change the course of our lives. Speechless but overwhelmed with emotions, we were thrilled, excited, and also scared. Our little boy now in Henrietta's arms, we were both fully aware of the responsibility we had just taken on of protecting, caring for, and nurturing this new little life.

RICHARD WILBUR

On July 5, 1986, the Statue of Liberty, which had been closed for repairs for the previous two years, was reopened to the public and re-dedicated. A few weeks earlier *LIFE* magazine had a photograph of the statue on its cover. I bought a copy and when I opened it, there was a poem on the inside cover written by Richard Wilbur.

I had been familiar with his name since the early sixties, having acted in professional productions of his masterful translations of Moliere plays: *The Misanthrope*, for which he had won the first of two Pulitzer Prizes, and *Tartuffe*. These plays are written entirely in rhyming couplets in French, and the rhyming words in French don't translate to words that rhyme in English, so to find an equivalent word without changing the meaning of the original is a monumental task. These are considered the definitive translations most often used in English-speaking productions.

He had been commissioned to write a poem for the re-dedication of The Statue of Liberty, which he titled, "On Freedom's Ground." It's quite a long poem set to the original music of composer William Schuman. The section of the poem on the inside of *LIFE* consisted of only sixteen lines, but they moved me deeply.

On the strength of this one excerpt, I looked up everything about his published poems. I purchased a book containing 250 of his poems entitled *New and Collected Poems*, for which he won his second Pulitzer Prize. After reading them all, I was so taken with them that I chose twenty poems from that collection to put together a forty-minute program that I titled, "A Journey Through the Mind of Richard Wilbur." It begins with a poem about birth, then one on childhood, then adolescence, his war years, his wife, his four children, and other poems about his philosophy of life.

I'd been giving piano concerts at various retirement homes around the Los Angeles area and thought this would be another excellent diversion for the retirees. Writing to the publishers of the book, Harcourt, Brace, Jovanovich, I told them the poems I intended to use and asked about royalty fees I would need to pay in to perform them publicly. I also included my credentials as an actor and mentioned my great admiration for Mr. Wilbur's work and that I'd acted in three productions of his Moliere translations. They wrote back, "Thirty dollars for each poem, however, there are three of the twenty that you've chosen, that only Mr. Wilbur owns the rights to. We will forward your letter with your request to his home in Cummington, Massachusetts."

Calculating thirty dollars times twenty amounting to six hundred dollars for each public performance, made my plan prohibitive. I dropped the idea. These poems are so inspiring to me that while I ran around Central Park every other day, I would carry a few of his poems with me and eventually had all twenty memorized. I loved ruminating on them while I ran.

About a week after I sent my request to Mr. Wilbur's publishers, I received the most beautiful letter from Cummington, Massachusetts, from Mr. Wilbur himself:

Dear Mr. Towey,

Harcourt Brace's permissions people have forwarded to me your letter of 12 June, in which you asked for performance rights to a number of my poems. I'm very happy that you wish to do a program of my work for retires of Southern California, and you have my permission to make use of any poems of mine which suit your purpose—and without paying any permission's fees.

Many good wishes to you,

Then he signed his name, Richard Wilbur, in pen.

This letter is framed and has been sitting on my desk for a long time. We carried on a pen pal relationship on and off for the next twenty-five years until he died at the age of ninety-six in the year 2017. I have many postcards from him and a few letters. They are all typed on the same old-fashioned typewriter. All the lower case *e*'s are filled with ink in that little half circle at the top of the letter. Since almost all his poems appeared in the *New Yorker* magazine before they were compiled into one of his many published books of poetry, he would often drop a line with a heads-up to me saying, "This one"— and he'd give the title of the poem and the date of weekly publication before it appeared on the newsstands—"I think this one might suit your acting purposes. Again, feel free to use it if it fits your program." We never met, but I was always astounded and humbled that I was carrying on a correspondence with this giant of the literary world.

Our wives passed away in the same year, 2007, both from complications of Alzheimer's disease. In this letter, and always on his personal stationery with his name boldly printed in deep blue at the top, he would type his full Massachusetts address, then:

Dear John Towey,

That photograph on your wife's memorial program is utterly beautiful and full of life, and I am honored that my little milkweed poem should be included. (He doesn't capitalize the name "Milkweed" in this letter as it always is in his books). The program, together with that of your recent piano concert, tells me what a wonderful thirty-some years you shared in the performing arts.

I too am no longer a caregiver, my wife having died a few months ago. After 64 years, I still am warmed and cheered by her presence, but stabbed at times by her absence. No doubt your friends, like mine, advised you to "keep busy," and I have been translating play after play of Corneille, and hoping to be visited by poems.
I send you many good wishes

And then, as always, he would sign his full name with a pen.

When I decided to include his "Milkweed" poem in Henrietta's memorial program, it was too late to write and ask his permission to use it, but when I sent the program to him, I apologized for printing it without asking his permission.

When I would sit down to write to him, before I could put pen to paper, and because he was such a giant in the literary world, I had to pretend that he hadn't won two Pulitzer Prizes, hadn't translated Moliere plays, hadn't written the lyrics to Bernstein's "Candide," wasn't named Poet Laureate of the United States, and hadn't been the recipient of a myriad of prestigious poetry awards. I would have to say out loud to myself, "Be honest! *Come on*, just speak from your heart." There were three poems that used to start my heart when I would begin saying them. "Why don't you tell him that?" I thought. So I did. He was always very kind in his responses.

One of his poems, which again appeared in the *New Yorker* called "The Censor," a short eight-line poem, has such a surprise in the last line that when I read it, I began laughing so hard I fell off the kitchen chair I'd been sitting on. I said to myself, "No, you can't tell him that." And then I'd say, "Yes, you can. Write to him and tell him," so I did. On a postcard he wrote back, among other things: "I'm delighted with your response to, The Censor."

He was always very faithful in responding to anything that I'd write to him. Months would go by and I wouldn't write, but when I did, within a week I would always receive a card or letter from him. I was always thrilled to receive anything from him. The last postcard he sent said, among other things, "Tell your retirees that at 93 I'm still teaching, but only one class a week; poetry on Friday afternoons at Vassar."

An actor and poet living here at MPTF, Harry Northup, approached me the other day in the library here on campus, after I'd told him weeks before about my love of the poetry of Richard Wilbur, and tapping me on the shoulder said, "I belong to a poetry organization called Beyond Baroque that is housed in the old City Hall building in Venice, California, and in March of 2021 it will be the centennial of Richard Wilbur's birth. Why don't you do your program about him down there that year as a tribute to him?"

Thank you," I said, "That's a great idea. I'm going to try to arrange that."

It's been a couple of years since he's passed, but I still miss, and will always miss the unusual and yet somehow personal relationship we had together.

CARPE DIEM

That is my muse: *Carpe Diem*, "Seize the Day." Throughout the years, I have made many signs with those words printed in large letters that I've placed strategically, slightly hidden but accessible, throughout the various apartments and homes where I've lived as a constant reminder. My favorite scene in Peter Weir's film *Dead Poet's Society* takes place in the sports trophy room where Robin Williams, who is teaching at a private boy's school, takes his twenty students on their first day of class and asks one of the boys to read "To the Virgins, to Make Much of Time" by Robert Herrick, aloud.

The Latin sentiment for this quatrain is *Carpe Diem*. Seize the Day. Mr. Williams says, "We are food for worms, boys. One day we will stop breathing, turn cold and die."

Then he shows the students the photo of a school football team in a glass case from years past. Everyone on the team is smiling. "These boys are now fertilizing daffodils," he says. He asks the boys to lean in closer to the photo. "If you lean in a little closer you can hear them whisper *Carpe Diem*." He repeats it again in a whisper, "*Carpe Diem*. Seize the Day. Make your lives extraordinary."

I was the same age as the students were in this film when my father would ask me to help him pick up dead bodies. He and his brother owned and operated The Towey Funeral Home in Rochester, Minnesota, that their father, my grandfather, had begun in the mid-1920s. "Always lift with your legs, John, not with your back," my father would instruct me as we picked up a cadaver from a hospital morgue or a private home. During my teenage years, I went on many of these trips with my dad and many times in the middle of the night. I didn't realize until years later that he was grooming me to take over the business.

The first time I accompanied my father on one of these trips, I remember the dead man was in his late middle age, but on seeing this dead body, the first I'd ever seen, I suddenly had a visceral feeling and a vivid awareness of being alive. As a teenager, one forgets the fact that eventually you're going to die, but every time I picked up a corpse, that feeling of aliveness would rush through me. The body would be placed in the hearse and taken to the funeral home. Then placed on a special table in the embalming room. I watched my father do this embalming procedure many times. When he needed extra help with a funeral, I would deliver flowers from the funeral home to the church, drive relatives to the church, then to the cemetery, and often take many bouquets of flowers to various nursing homes after the funeral.

My father saw my interest in theater begin in high school and he and my mother drove to a distant college in northern Minnesota several times to watch me perform. During the summer, I acted and directed in a barn outside of Rochester that a bunch of us gutted and turned into the Rochester Summer Theatre. The man who ran the local civic theatre in town, who was a graduate of the Goodman School of Drama in Chicago, saw my work in many of these plays and felt that I could possibly make a career in the theater. He spoke to my father about this and a few weeks later, this man and his wife drove me to Chicago to see the school and meet several of the teachers. I applied, was accepted, and entered the school the next semester.

My father pointed out to me that there were many professional men and women in Rochester—doctors, lawyers, etc.—that satisfied their "acting bug" by working at the local civic theater occasionally, while still maintaining their businesses.

Among many other duties, a funeral director must deal constantly with people who are in a state of grief. To acquire a license to become a funeral director, one must have two years of college along with a specific subject called "The Psychology of Grief." I greatly admired my father having observed his skill at dealing with families in various emotional states of grief.

My father and his brother had made a very good living going into business with my grandfather. They both had homes on a hill in town called Pill Hill that acquired this designation because many of the doctors that worked at the local Mayo Clinic lived there. Knowing that I could have inherited the business that had been running smoothly for decades, there was the thought that I'd be dealing with grieving families for the rest of my working life. One other problem: my father and his brother were alcoholics. High-functioning alcoholics, but alcoholics. They were not near retirement age which meant I'd have to be working with them for many years if I decided to take over the business. Although we never spoke of it, my father knew when I went off to school in Chicago that I'd given up any thought of succeeding him in the funeral business. But he and my mother backed me all the way with my career choice and when I came into their living rooms on a television soap opera several times a week, two years after leaving school, they were thrilled.

We can
remember
correctly and
still
misunderstand.

DEBORAH ROGOSIN

MY FOUR MEN

Floating in and out of my dreams with the men I've loved. I love friends and family, but this kind of love is deep, extra special and enduring.

Riding on the shoulders of my dad and dancing standing on his feet. His reactive smiles warm my heart. Always telling me how smart I was, how cute I was and how I was going to make my husband a very proud man one day. Always looking at me warm and loving.

Ron, my brother, my teacher, my protector. He taught me how to read from comic books before I started school. Sweet Ron stood between me and my mean brother Ernie in pictures and sitting in the car, he'd seat Ernie by one window and me at the opposite side, with the other two children in the middle, so I wouldn't get pinched. He'd take me for a ride on his bicycle if I needed something. He'd give me money from his paper route. He helped with math. I'd tease him about his girlfriend and say, "Tosca Rovetti, she eats mashed spaghetti." He would only smile at me.

When he was in high school, he'd have me comb his hair before he put on his hat and played the clarinet in the marching band. We were in touch all of our lives until he died last November. The last time I saw him he looked in my eyes and said:

"Life begins and ends with love." I loved him all of my life.

My father-in-law, an administrative law judge for the NLRB, was so intelligent and charming. He adored me and I loved him. He went back to his first love, the theater, after he and my mother-in-law, Helen, retired to Palm Springs. We took a bus load of friends to see him perform in a play and surprised him. He was a wonderful actor, but his mother and sister had insisted that he become a lawyer. He lived with us after his wife died the last five years of his life. He was so neat and clean. He was one of the kindest men I ever met. I couldn't do enough for him. We never disagreed except about broccoli, which he hated. He called it little trees, He would only eat it to please me and because I said it was good for him. In the evenings he'd recite poetry for me: "The Highwayman," "Lasca," and "Jenny Kissed Me." He wrote me a moving love letter before he died.

And then there's Joel, the love of my life, who I love every minute of the day; kind, witty, charming, always generous, sexy, intelligent, creative and so many popular positive adjectives I could put in front of his name. Joel gave me three beautiful daughters, He gave me my first bicycle on my twenty-seventh birthday all wrapped up with a bow and it was standing in the middle of the living room when I awoke that morning. Always so considerate. Always kind and oh so thoughtful, and I cherish him deeply with all my heart. He always invited me to go on locations with him. He has been so giving of appropriate gifts and arranged lovely vacations and some filled with surprises . . . Besides our trips in the United States, we have traveled to thirty-two countries. He never lied to me and we've always felt very close, more each year. Even when he gets annoyed, I say something that cracks him up and makes him laugh. If I lost him, there would never be another man that would compare or take Joel's place.

I continue to dream about these four men every night, have conversations, go on adventures, discuss problems of the day and times, and I am so lucky to have the ones passed on, in my life and now in memory, and my dreams! And I'll treasure every moment I have with my terrific husband.

The first three are gone now, but not in my heart, and still live in my thoughts and imagination.

One day, when I was walking to the gym, I was in the crosswalk with my guide dog, Asha, and a car came careening around the corner. Asha pushed me back out of the way while the driver yelled, "What's the matter, you stupid broad, are you blind or something?!" He sped off so quickly he didn't hear my response . . .

Looking back, when I was thirty-five years old, I received a master's degree in art. Ironically, that same week during a routine eye examination, I was diagnosed with Retinitis Pigmentosa (RP) a rare recessive genetic eye condition which could lead to blindness over time. Much to my surprise, the doctor told me that my central vision was good, but my overall visual range was limited to 20 percent. I guess I was accustomed to scanning a lot and didn't notice my gradual loss. A 20-percent field of vision is considered legally blind. I realized that my art degree would not serve me well under the circumstances. After a blue funk, some soul searching, and therapy, I went back to school to become a psychotherapist.

My first internship was at the Foundation for the Junior Blind in Los Angeles, in the mid-seventies. Under the supervision of a psychologist, I worked with recently blinded adults, blind children and their families. Among the many skills I learned was teaching others to accommodate to their new visually-impaired situation. From working with this population, I learned a tremendous amount, which would serve me well in the future, especially when I lost most of my vision ten or fifteen years ago. I continue to learn daily.

Helping people adjust to sudden vision loss and working with multi-handicapped children and their families, I understand that blind people are not necessarily "disabled," but have many abilities. I have met blind teachers, lawyers and even doctors. I was very surprised to meet a blind ophthalmologist. Yes, he did have a sighted assistant. But he knew his stuff! Stevie Wonder and Ray Charles are successful despite of their blindness, as is hotel entrepreneur, Steve Wynn, who also happens to have RP. I've met blind people who have traveled the world alone, including entertainer Tom Sullivan, who is known to surf and ski, and once was able to save his son from drowning.

As the second millennium approached and my vision narrowed significantly, I decided to get a guide dog. I did my research and discovered that I had to have a great deal more mobility instruction with a cane before that could happen. I also needed to be trained with the dog every day, with a trainer, for a full month. After all, the blind person needs to learn to direct the dog, not the other way around. Sometimes, though, you might have a dog who seems smarter than the master. I thought I did, with my first dog Gina, a beautiful reddish golden retriever. We would come out of an office building or medical center and if the driver had forgotten where we parked, I would say, "Gina, find the car," and she would take us directly to it. She was the one dog who in some ways was smarter than both of us.

I'm currently living on the campus of the Motion Picture Television Fund, where I can easily navigate in "pitch darkness" so that I can access many of the activities available here. I've noticed that some of the residents and staff are hesitant to assist a blind person. Other people, who mean well, make inappropriate suggestions. It's interesting how little others know about guide dogs and mobility training. Repeatedly, people tell me to walk in the middle of the path rather than on the side, but I am guided by the edges and landmarks. I find an object or a step with my cane. That way, I can feel what is ahead two or three feet, sweeping the cane from left to right as I step forward. Occasionally, when I approach a bush or other obstacle, someone yells, "You're going to run into a bush!" Friends are trying to protect me, but they don't understand that I'm using those landmarks to find my way.

I use the same methods inside a room, following edges and objects to guide me. I recall one gentleman who used to slip past me as I went to the dining room restroom, so he could turn the light on for me in advance. He did this several times, trying to be helpful. But the light doesn't make a darn bit of difference. I need to learn my way around by touch. Sometimes I just want to say, "Thank you," and I do appreciate people's good intentions.

People often ask how they can help me. Usually, I have it covered. When I do need help, I'm quick to ask for it. Remember, a friendly tone is always good, as well as a clear, direct question. Of course, I don't see your hand gestures and I can't benefit from eye contact. Frequently, if I ask the location of something, people say it's over there and point towards it. A better method is to say, "Is there anything I can help you with?" Always be clear and precise when giving directions.

If you are guiding me, a friendly arm can be offered. That is especially helpful if you are taking me to an unfamiliar location, such as a room inside a medical office. If you're guiding someone, be aware of what's in front of them, so they don't trip over anything, and you don't walk them into a wall or a low tree branch. If the space ahead becomes narrow, tell the person or simply move your elbow back a few inches, and they will walk behind you. At times, too much chatter about obstacles ahead can distract the blind person, who is trying to focus on navigation. Some people tell me every little turn they take, but being guided feels more like dancing, and it's unnecessary to offer a lot of detail unless there is a very sharp, sudden turn ahead. It is important, though, to mention any upcoming steps and to stop before each curb. There is nothing more annoying than being pushed, clutched or pulled across a street. I'm sure you can imagine.

On occasion, when I go to a restaurant, the waitress asks my husband, "What would she like for lunch?" His answer is always, "Ask her!" Because a person is blind doesn't mean they are stupid, deaf, or unable to talk or think for themselves. I've had more than one person yell in my ear to communicate, since they see I am carrying a white cane. I do have a partial loss of hearing in one ear, but I'm not deaf.

During my internship, there was a young blind teenager ahead of me as I was rushing to an appointment. She always wanted to stop and talk. This time, I decided I would disguise my footsteps so she would not recognize me. I was in a hurry that day, so I pretended to limp. She called out to me, "What happened to your foot, Deborah?" True enough, a blind person does start to know people's footsteps. While our hearing does not improve with blindness, we do learn to focus more on other senses.

I'm pretty good with voices, and I've certainly memorized a lot of voices here. But some people expect me to remember them after identifying themselves to me just once. They like to make a game of it, asking me what their name is. I used to guess, but now I just say, "Daffy Duck!" I appreciate it when new people tell me their names the first several times we meet. Then, I'm more likely to remember them in the future.

So basically, it's quite simple to help a blind person, if you want to do that. Ask if they need any help or offer them your arm if the situation presents itself. Don't correct what they're trying to do unless you see imminent danger, like a rattlesnake in front of them. Be specific, without using hand gestures or pointing and saying, "It's over there." If, on the other hand, you see me walking toward a twenty-foot pothole in the street, yell, "DEBORAH, STOP!" before I fall in!

Remember that blindness could happen to you some day, and as Norm Kaplan, the director of the Foundation for the Junior Blind, used to say, "It's nice to be nice." In this case, "nice" means friendly, thoughtful, and considerate—and not just considering the person's disability, but also their ability.

DINNER IN THE DARK

After Joel's retirement and before moving to the Country House at the Motion Picture Television Fund, we lived in Oxnard. When Joel lost his ability to drive at night, preventing us from going to Friday night services at the synagogue, we joined the Unitarian Church. It was close to our home and we really enjoyed the services and the people involved. There were Christians, Jews, mixed Jewish/Christian marriages, Jack Catholics, Buddhists and Mormons, agnostics and atheists in the congregation. There was also an LGBT group. Overall it was a highly educated, interesting and varied community, and most welcoming. Everyone spent a lot of time doing charity work, feeding the homeless, helping flood victims, and so on. We made many friends.

I wanted to come up with some kind of fundraiser, and I wanted it to be creative and personal. I had always enjoyed cooking and entertaining, so I hosted a "Dinner in the Dark," to help people understand how I operate as a blind person.

We planned a gourmet dinner for eight and charged a donation of eighty dollars for each guest. We started the evening with greetings and champagne. When it was time to sit at the table, we gathered in the dining room, and everyone put on eye masks except me. The guests all wore their masks throughout the meal, guessing what each food was. Our son-in-law, Jon, helped with the last minute cooking and our daughter, Robin, served everyone, so I could stay at the table.

The first course was stuffed mushrooms, then minestrone soup, my personal recipe. Our guests all knew what the mushrooms were, but couldn't guess the soup until one man said, "Minestrone! I just tasted a bean." For the next course there was a delicate salad of arugula, candied pecans and pomegranate seeds, with sesame dressing, then a butternut squash enchilada with tomatillo sauce. After that, the guests were presented with the main course: a portion of marinated baked salmon, or filet if they preferred beef, my favorite vegetable concoction, and asparagus marinated in Asian dressing. We served an appropriate wine with each course.

For dessert I had some pretty little crystal dessert dishes with three small compartments. I filled the sections with chocolate mousse, my special flan and zesty lemon sherbet. After dinner I served an after-dinner liqueur. All the servings were small, and everyone ate every bite on their plate, guessing what it was. The conversation flowed, and we laughed a lot.

When dinner was over, we went into the living room and passed around common household objects that each person had to identify by touch. Some of them were difficult to recognize blindfolded, like an egg timer, cheese grater, and a sock mender. I tried to find things that weren't obvious.

Then I shared some of my assistive technology devices for the blind with our guests. We went into the kitchen and I demonstrated my labeling machine for identifying herbs, spices, prescriptions, and more. I would place the machine on a small sticker on the jar and record what it was in my own voice, and then push another button to read it. I also shared a variety of other tools, including my talking computer, my color identifier, and the Victor Stream device that records my books to read audibly.

I repeated the party as a fundraiser for several years, and it attracted increasing numbers of people, eager to participate. We chose to limit the guest list to eight each time. Most everyone followed the rules and kept their eyes covered, but once we noticed a psychiatrist taking an occasional peek over his mask, and another time a friend had to remove her mask early because it made her feel claustrophobic.

This event suited me well, because it allowed me to educate others so they could learn how a blind person manages basic skills. It also helped participants to overcome their perceptions of the limitations of blindness. There are so many strategies and tools that help me navigate the world, and I was happy to share them with others.

One year, the *Ventura Star* newspaper came to interview me about my party, and the article is probably still online. After the article was published, I noticed several other groups—including a chapter of the National Association for the Blind and Guide Dogs of America— hosting similar events.

I do miss entertaining and sometimes I get a strong yen to cook once again. I still enjoy cooking for special events, with my family. And, while I miss my connections at the Unitarian Church in Oxnard, I have made many new friends here in our MPTF community.

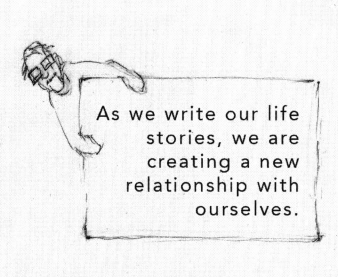

As we write our life
stories, we are
creating a new
relationship with
ourselves.

SANDY BOLLINGER

BASEBALL

Growing up in New York, every Sunday my uncles would come for bagels and lox and a shouting match. I would listen to my father and uncles carry on about whose baseball teams were the best.

My father was a die-hard Dodger fan, Uncle Phil, a Giants fan and Uncle Lou, a devout Yankee fan.

My father owned his own taxi and when the Dodgers played at Ebbets field, he would be waiting when the game was over, to pick up players and enjoyed gabbing with them about the game. It was the highlight of his day.

My mother detested baseball and the bickering that took place in her kitchen. She couldn't wait to leave the house, taking my sister Jane and I out after the men were fed.

All my childhood I remember her yelling at Dad when he was involved in a baseball game. He paid no attention to her yelling—he had a transistor radio glued to his ear to hear the commentary and he watched the game on TV at the same time. He wasn't about to miss anything.

Meanwhile, upset that Dad spent most of his day glued to the game, she let my sister and I know how much she resented baseball.

My father had wanted a son to play ball with and share his passion for baseball. Instead he got two adoring daughters. After I married and had children, a girl and two boys, he was overjoyed! Finally grandsons to share his love of baseball.

Unfortunately, that was not the case. Neither of my boys were into sports. They competed in gymnastics, swim teams and loved to dance. Sissies, my father called them, but he still showered them with love.

When my daughter Jennifer married Dave, as big a sports nut as my father, my dad found the son he was waiting for.

Dave would take my dad to baseball games, watch it on TV with him, and they would discuss all the plays and hash over the game. Finally, someone who understood him.

My grandsons were born with baseball mitts on their hands. Both started playing sports before they were born.

They knew all the teams, and who played on which team and any statistic about any player from the time they were eight years old.

Unfortunately, my father passed away before he could get to know his great-grandsons and kvell over their athletic ability. The boys played many sports but chose to excel at baseball.

Well, Dad, you would not believe what Mom and I did. Being loving grandmother and great-grandmother, we showed up at almost every sport the boys played in. Even when Mom was in a wheelchair, we rolled her to the games.

We couldn't believe we went to baseball games and cheered and yelled just like you did. Once I was about to jump up and scream at the ump when he made a bad call. Oh my, I was turning into my father.

When our grandson, Shawn, was about six and in Little League, he hit the ball very hard. After the game, I said to him, "I can't wait to tell Grandpa Isie how well you played. He would have been so excited to watch you."

Shawn looked up at me with a puzzled expression on his face, and said, "You know, Grandma, he is dead. Can he hear you?"

It took all I could do to keep from laughing and said, "I don't know if he can hear, but just in case he can, I always talk to him about how well you and Jerry play. You are just what he was waiting for."

After one particular good game, I told him, when he is playing at Dodger Stadium, I want to sit down where all the important people sit.

Without blinking an eye, he said, "When I'm playing for the Dodgers, you'll be sitting up in the special booth." Even at a ripe old age of ten, he believed he would get to play for the Dodgers.

Over the years, Henri and I enjoyed traveling with their teams throughout the United States to watch them play in Little League games, Cooperstown, and the Macabee Games. Their teams won many championships and Shawn was voted MVP many times.

I even began watching baseball on television and reading the sports page so I could keep up to date when the boys quizzed me.

Shawn was recruited in his junior year of high school to play shortstop for Northwestern University. I just returned from Arizona where he played in his first college baseball game.

What a thrill for this old grandma, and I still talk to my father about how Shawn may one day play at Dodger Stadium.

THE FAMILY HONEYMOON

Have you ever been asked to join your children on their honeymoon? You would be correct if you said NO!

Who in their right mind would want their parents on their honeymoon! Well, our daughter Jennifer and her husband Dave did just that!

It all began when Jennifer and Dave met at UCLA law school. They had been dating about five years. When our telephone rang and Henri answered, it was Dave calling to see if he could come and talk to us. We pondered what it was, but secretly we both hoped it was about proposing to our daughter.

Indeed, that was what he wanted to talk about. He asked if he could marry our daughter and when we hugged and kissed him, he got his answer.

Then he explained that when his father was dying, he asked his wife to put her engagement ring aside for Dave when he got engaged. He wanted him to give the ring to his fiancée. It wasn't a big diamond and Dave wanted to know if we thought it was a good idea. All of Jennifer's friends had expensive, large diamond engagement rings. We looked at Dave and both exclaimed, "You don't know Jennifer very well, she would never wear a large diamond and she would be honored and thrilled to have a ring that your dad bought for your mom." He asked us not to say anything about it until he found a special way and time to ask her.

We kept waiting for Jennifer to tell us she was engaged. Months went by and not a word. They went to New York for New Years Eve to be with friends, and we waited up all night to see if that's where he would propose there. No phone call. They went to Washington, DC to visit his sister's family. He felt he finally found the right time to propose. He had arranged with the airline to have the stewardess put the ring on Jennifer's lunch tray with a note, "Will you marry me?" The ring was burning a hole in his pocket. He was feeling anxious. When they got to the airport the flight was canceled—and so was his plan. Now how would he go about it?! His sister suggested they visit the Smithsonian museum and when they get to the Hope Diamond, he should pull out his ring and say, "How about this one?" We got a call immediately.

They had wanted a small wedding; what they ended up with was 300 people.

They had so many friends and we both had large families and many friends.

It was a magical wedding reception. And now the honeymoon plans.

When Jennifer came to us with the absurd offer to join them on their honeymoon cruise, we looked at her with blank expressions on our faces. We couldn't believe what we had just heard.

Whoever heard of parents going on a honeymoon with their child?!

She explained that Dave's grandparents were going on an Alaskan cruise after the wedding and taking Dave's sister and husband. They offered to take Jennifer and Dave also. Dave told them he didn't think Jennifer would want to spend her honeymoon with his grandparents. They suggested he talk it over with Jennifer to see if she was willing to delay their honeymoon a week. She agreed, and he suggested they ask us to come also. A way to thank us for the wedding.

Henri and I felt it was a crazy idea and said no. Then Dave came and persuaded us to go. Dave insisted that we join them. He said we could get to know his family, and he and Jen could have some time alone.

The story gets even weirder. My cousins from New York were coming to the wedding. They had planned a trip after the wedding and wanted us to go with them. When I asked where they were going, I gasped, "Oh, no!" when they said on an Alaskan cruise. I asked the name of the ship, and lo and behold, the same one we were going on.

I told her about this incredible honeymoon journey. Joan immediately offered to cancel their plans. "Call Jennifer and tell her before you cancel."

"Of course," Jennifer replied, "you shouldn't change your plans, come and join us. The more the merrier." The grandparents booked the family on the opposite side of the ship from Jennifer and Dave. It was a large ship, but my cousins stateroom ended up next door to Jennifer and Dave.

It was just as Dave had hoped. We got to know some of his wonderful family.

We all enjoyed being together, except Dave, who felt ill and slept in his room most of the cruise. Jennifer acknowledged how fortunate she was to have us all to keep her company on her "alone" honeymoon.

Nothing that was
given to me is
mine to keep.

HENRI BOLLINGER

MY JOURNEY

My life began in a small town in Beyne-Heusay, Belgium. I was born to Luzer and Sarah Rosalie Bollinger. I had a sister, Paulette, who was born two years before.

My father was born in Stari-Sambor, a town in the Ukraine and left home at age thirteen to join a circus. When in the army, he was captured and sent to Siberia. As a prisoner of war, the commandant of the place was a Japanese who learned that my father was a chess player. He had my father play with him every day, and that saved his life.

When he returned to his home town, his brother asked if he would like to play chess with the guests at a resort where he was going to teach dancing to the owner's daughters. The owner was looking for a husband for his oldest daughter. My father was short and the daughter rejected him. My mother spoke up and said she wanted to marry him. She wanted out of the small community and knew my father was a world traveler.

They married and my father left to find work in other countries. When he landed work in Belgium, he sent for his wife. They lived in Beyne-Heusay, a small coal-mining community outside of Liege and near the German border.

The Germans had already launched World War II in Eastern Europe, destroying the armed forces of nations that were unprepared for the violence of the well-trained German army. Most European nations' defenses collapsed in a matter of days. Facing total annihilation, they quickly surrendered. The German Luftwaffe fielded two of the best fighters in all of World War II—the Messerschmitt Bf 109 and Focke-Wulf 190. The German Luftwaffe was created in the early 1930s, long before the start of World War II. Its intent was barring access to the United States by American and British warships.

When German Jews realized that they were in grave danger, they crossed the German border illegally. They would show up at local police stations and churches seeking protection. Our parents became a point of contact since they were the only Jews in the town. My mother learned of the atrocities going on in Germany and urged the rabbi of the synagogue in Liege which we attended to gather as many temple members as possible and leave immediately.

They organized groups to travel together across France where the local priest would help them find safe passage to ports in the south from which they could sail to safer havens such as England, South Africa, and the United States. They had to find seating on trains and buses to travel across France and by foot. Thousands of refugees were now on the move, including our family, the rabbi, and many other families. Trains and buses were under constant machine gun attacks from Messerschmitts.

My mother was hit in the upper leg and had to be taken to a hospital where they removed a bullet from the wound. She nevertheless insisted to continue on foot. My father carried two suitcases, one containing two Torahs and the other filled with clothing. My sister lugged a suitcase filled with clothing and I carried a somewhat smaller suitcase with additional clothing.

There were already too many U-boats trawling the Atlantic Ocean barring access to the United States, so Liverpool became our only option. Thousands of people were already seeking all forms of transportation to escape the fast-moving German army trying to board ships headed west when we arrived in Liverpool. It seemed to be a hopeless effort, but my parents were not ready to give up too easily, nor were the French, who were not eager to increase the number of Jewish residents within their country.

The cost of passage per person was also beyond my parents' means. However, working through a number of Jewish organizations that had emerged with the rise of Nazism to provide guidance and financing, thousands of Jews were able to escape which otherwise would not have been possible. Many of us had to sleep on bunks on the ships' decks which turned out to be a good summer camp–like experience for the children.

When I landed in England in the spring of 1940, I was soon to celebrate my ninth birthday. I had experienced at this young age more drama than most children do in a lifetime!

The ship landed in Southampton where various religious, charitable, and social organizations assisted with the legal process for these new refugees. We children faced challenges we never previously encountered, such as learning a new language and a plethora of basic approaches to dealing with simple classroom topics. In retrospect, it's amazing how quickly we overcame them.

I recall my first day of an English course when the teacher spoke French. "I'd like to welcome a new student, Henri Bollinger, who just arrived from Belgium, my home country," she said. She continued speaking in French. "Henri, this is the last time you will hear French spoken during this course if you expect to get a response from me."

I learned to speak conversational English in less than two months!

My parents' anxiety grew over our safety as bombing increased in different parts of England on a daily basis. They had us return to London where they felt that they had better control over our safety. They felt that spending nights in underground subway stations offered better protection, so we packed clothes and headed back to London.

Every evening we would pack some clothes and food and head to the underground station where we joined hundreds of other families for what became a daily routine. The loud sounds of exploding bombs could be heard through the night and offered a clue as to the seriousness of the latest attack which we could confirm the next morning as we headed home through the rubble of destroyed homes, shops, and office buildings. Our daily routine began after breakfast. As soon as we got home from our overnight stay in the underground station, we changed into our school uniform and began our daily routine.

Our parents were quite excited about educational opportunities now that we were in London. My mother had developed a talent for creating works of art through crocheting when growing up in Poland. She sold some of her creations to neighbors in an enterprising way. Now that we were in a big city, she saw an opportunity to teach her new neighbors the art of turning household goods, such as pillowcases, bedspreads, and curtains, as works of art. She would buy skeins of multiple colors from wholesales in downtown Liege.

Word spread throughout the neighborhood and Madame Bollinger was soon developing a following. One of my father's favorite weekend activities was to photograph winning horses and riders at the local race track. Accompanying my dad became a regular weekend activity which I shared whenever my mother would let me. My father also found ways to earn extra money when he noticed that several people were taking photos of the winning horses and riders. He got excited when he heard that they were paid for copies of each photo sold. He bought an inexpensive camera that allowed him to take and process photos on the spot.

Once we got resettled in London, with the help of Chaim Weitzman's organization, formed to assist Jewish refugees, selecting appropriate schools for the children became a priority. My mother joined that organization and lobbied to get her daughter into St. Martin's School of Art, England's most highly regarded art institute. My sister went on to teach art in London and at the Fashion Institute in New York after we came to the US.

I already had other ideas! Since my early childhood, our parents took us to see Jewish plays and musicals and to movie houses to see the latest movies. I was hooked! I insisted that I'd prefer to study theater, acting, and dance. I was enrolled at the Marion Ross School of Drama.

Marion Ross was the primary source for delivering young actors best prepared to meet the demands of the profession. After just a couple of months, I began to audition for both movies and theater productions. The auditioning process was a key part of the training we received. Getting "callbacks" was almost as exciting as actually landing a role.

Miss Ross also encouraged me to enroll in the Buddy Bradley School of Dance to further expand my job opportunities. Mr. Bradley, an African-American dancer, who gained attention in England and throughout Europe during the 1930s when tap dancing received worldwide attention when it was featured in a number of popular American movies by Bill "Bojangles" Robinson, Fred Astaire, and Gene Kelly. Mr. Bradley worked on many Broadway and West End shows. He was the first black dancer to choreograph an all-white show in London.

The result of all these efforts soon began to pay off. I was cast in a number of stage productions, including the national tour of Lillian Hellman's *Watch on the Rhine*. I also appeared in several movies. Most noteworthy was *Johnny Frenchman*, starring famed iconic French actress, Françoise Rosay, as well as a scene with Jean Simmons in David Lean's *Great Expectations*.

My studies at the Marion Ross School included the exploration of literary classics including the works of William Shakespeare, Francis Bacon, Moliere, Victor Hugo, Ben Jonson, William Wycherley, Oliver Goldsmith, Richard Sheridan, Oscar Wilde, and J. M. Synge.

It was these literary experiences that led me to a lifelong career in publicity. ✒

FBI INVESTIGATING HENRI BOLLINGER

The Cold War mentality was still rampant in the 1960s when I received a phone call from a neighbor to let me know that an FBI agent was knocking on door asking questions about us. We were stunned. Why would the FBI be investigating us?

When I got into my car to go to work the next morning, I noticed something on the floor that turned out to be an ear piece for a recording device. This was serious. Someone had broken into my car searching for evidence of some kind!

Then the call came directly from the FBI. They wanted to know why we were getting phone calls from behind the Iron Curtain in the middle of the night. Whew. It hit me.

I had recently taken on a new client, The Dobritch International Circus which represented most of the world's top circus acts, including trapeze artists the Great Wallandas, as well as amazing wild animal acts.

Al Dobritch, the gruff circus owner, lived in Bulgaria and called me at all hours, often in the wee hours of the morning, ignoring time differences.

After the taking-over of Bulgaria by the Communist Party in 1946, the Royal Dobritch Circus was nationalized. I suspected that Dobritch was under the control of the Bulgarian communist government and now, also of interest to the US intelligence services.

I represented *The Hollywood Palace*, the successful variety show which ran for seven years on ABC. Since they often used Dobritch's clients on their show, I felt obliged to let the show's producers know of these developments.

Al came to my office the next day and, in his brusk, burly way, told me he wanted me to get publicity for him and his circus. He invited my wife and I to dinner at the Beverly Wilshire Hotel to celebrate the occasion. We got there a touch early and there was a reservation for a table for twelve. He had invited eight other people I did not know and we never discussed what his expectations were nor what my fee would be.

He invited us to dinner again the next evening, at which time we made a deal, and the next day he flew back to Bulgaria. That's when the phone calls began. Fee payments were late. He said not to worry, he would pay when he returned to the US. He eventually came by my office and he pulled a wad of hundred-dollar bills from his pocket. He peeled off what we agreed to and said he always paid in cash.

When he brought his circus to Los Angeles, he invited our family to be his guests and to go backstage to meet the acts. Our young three-year-old daughter was thrilled to meet the clowns.

I never knew when and if I would get paid. He was very late paying and, during one of his early morning calls, he said someone would come by my office and pay me. Next day, a man shows up with a brown paper bag and empties the cash on my desk.

Dobritch was eccentric, to say the least. He also brought circus acts to Las Vegas, where he loved to gamble. I don't remember at what point we parted, but one day I read in the paper that Al Dobritch fell out a window at one of the downtown Las Vegas hotels on March 11, 1971. I remember saying to Sandy that he must have owed the mob a lot of money and felt that he could get away with it!

That's the last I ever heard of Dobritch or from the FBI. But he absolutely kept me from making decisions that seem too good to be true!!!

Memoir is as
much being told
as it is telling.

MICKEY COTTRELL

AN EXCERPT FROM *THE FIREMAN'S EQUIPMENT*

Beneath the willow tree in the Cottrells' side yard, we hear Mickey "reading" to Lila from the new comic. As we hear it, it's the story of "The Birdman of Heaven," more commonly known as "Captain Marvel." The little girl is indeed in heaven and when her story teller finishes, she leans over and gives him a quick kiss on the cheek. They both look surprised and embarrassed. "I don't know why I did that. I think it was the comic book," Lila says, attempting an explanation for what just transpired.

"Well, why don't you kiss it then?" the boy says, slapping her face with the comic.

"I like you too, Mickey," Lila offers, thinking though that the magic is really in the comic book.

An idea brewing, the boy jumps up. "Let's go to your house."

"Okay," says Lila and off they run.

In her frilly little girl's room, Lila sits on her bed with Mickey. She reintroduces him to all her dolls, who sit at attention on a long shelf on the opposite wall. Mickey's gaze keeps returning to the smart, little blonde one with "three changes of clothes—causal, dressy, and casual-dressy."

"I have an idea," Mickey offers. "I'll give you the 'Big Special Issue Comic' book, if you'll trade me 'Victoria with her three outfits' for it."

A profound silence falls upon the little room of ribbons, lace, and pastels. Mickey stares intently at Lila, who very seriously looks at all her dolls and tries to imagine the shelf without Victoria. Then she glances again at the comic book her friend is extending. Then back again. She is one torn apart little lady.

Mickey takes advantage of her perplexity. "You better say 'yes' before I change my mind."

Lila blinks her eyes a couple times and then jumps off the bed and climbs up to the shelf to bring down Victoria and her wardrobe. Mickey smiles.

Later, the two friends sit at either end of the front porch glider, she with her big comic and he with Victoria. Each is thoroughly oblivious of the other, lost in the wonder of their new treasures.

Mickey takes Victoria, in the appropriate outfit, of course, everywhere. Mother thinks it's very cute. So do her friends as the boy just talks away to his piece of plastic.

At the grocery, Mickey pushes the cart with Victoria in the infant seat. He tells his charge that he is not made of money so she can't have everything she wants, which are, of course, the most expensive things in the store. Mother and the grocer suppress a chuckle in the background. Victoria is dressed casual in a little blue and white cotton gingham dress.

At a grown-up party at Rodney's friend Gibby's parents' house, Mickey sits on the carpet "reading" Victoria a comic. They sit right in the middle of the action. Behind them is the coffee table, covered with dips 'n' chips, coasters, and cocktails, a silver cigarette box, and large ashtrays. In front of them is that most fascinating new gizmo, a television set with its small screen and huge cabinet. Daddy is standing at the set with the host, Stanley, but can't help but notice his son. He doesn't like what he sees, "This doll business." Mother and a lady friend are amused with "Mickey and Vicki."

Through the picture window, we see big brother Rodney and his friend Gibby in sweaters, firing a hardball into each other's glove. Stanley asks Jack if he's ever seen Milton Berle's show on TV.

"No, but I did see the Yankees play the Dodgers on Jake Harper's TV. Jean is very opposed to getting one. Thinks we'll stop talking to each other and camp out in front of it 'round the clock."

"She doesn't have to worry about that just yet," Stanley clarifies. "There are only a few shows on everyday at this point, but even Dizzy Dean's talking about doing his games live on TV next year."

"Yeah, I know," Jack responds. "That could be great." But Daddy's distracted by his son and the doll. "I'm gonna get another drink, Stanley."

"Sure, help yourself." The host gestures towards the kitchen as a couple approaches him to ask about the TV set.

Daddy leaves the room. Mickey doesn't notice and Victoria, of course, is wearing her party dress, pearl necklace, and her mock "mink" stole. Mother made the necklace out of tiny white beads strung on thread.

The proud "parent," bundled up in a red jacket and scarf, is eating a cheeseburger and drinking a Shirley Temple on the flagstone patio outside the main dining room at the Bayou de Sirde Country Club. Rodney and Mickey's best friend, Owen, are also at the table lunching. Gibby comes over, noticing the doll, who is in her own chair, wearing the casual-dressy outfit, Mickey's favorite—yellow pedal pushers, high heels, and a pink blouse with an upturned collar, tied pirate-style, exposing her midriff. Mother also made a little coordinated yellow chiffon scarf for what she calls, "Victoria's lovely long neck."

"Isn't that pretty queer," Gibby whispers to Roddy, "a boy playin' with a doll?"

"Lay off," big brother responds. "He's only five. He deosn't have to hit a home run and drive a truck for a couple more years yet, Gib."

"I dunno," the unconvinced friend responds.

The black waiter with salt and pepper hair in a crisp white jacket comes over to the table. "Is there anything else I can bring you fine young gentlemen?"

"No, thanks, Jackson. We're fine," Roddy replies.

"Jackson," Mickey asks, "can you please bring another straw for Victoria?"

"Sure 'nuff, Mr. Mickey. With pleasure."

Daddy and a couple golfer friends round the corner just below the patio, their black caddies carrying clubs behind them. They're on their way to the tenth hole. "Hi, kids," Daddy smiles and waves, uncharacteristically happy.

"He must be winning," Mickey notes.

Rodney spurts out a bit of burger as he explodes with laughter.

Daddy pauses, talking to his partner and then decides to wash a couple of golf balls in the nearby apparatus.

He steps to the ball washer, in earshot of the kids, when Jackson returns with the paper straw for Victoria. Bowing at the waist and handing it to Mickey, Jackson enthuses, "And I reckon, Miss Victoria is the best dressed lady at the club today."

"You think?" Mickey asks.

"No doubt about it, that girl's a debutante," Jackson assures.

The other three boys chuckle. Mickey just smiles proudly and adjusts her scarf.

Jackson spots Mr. Cottrell below at the ball washer. "Afternoon, Mr. Jack. Your boys are growin' into fine young men, sir."

"I'm glad you think so, Jackson. Rodney's coming along, but I don't know about the other one." Daddy tosses one ball to his caddie and tosses to other one in the air on his way to the tee.

Jackson puts his hand on Mickey's shoulder, who is clearly hurt. "Don't think nothin' of it, Mr. Mickey. He must be losin'."

Gibby shoots Roddy an I-told-ya-so glance.

Christmas Eve at the Cottrell home. Momma and her two sons are excited and happy as they take their seats around the tree, which is surrounded by dozens of presents. Daddy grumbles softly, "Goddammit" and walks to an open closet, closing the door. "I'm not paying to heat this closet."

The family opens their presents. Daddy films the occasion with the new 8mm Bell & Howell camera he's given himself. Mother models her new stole with little foxes biting onto each other's tails. She's very happy.

Through his new camera, Daddy looks to Roddy who's balancing a football on his finger and a basketball on his head, then to Mickey, who turns around smiling, holding up four dolls. Daddy turns off the camera, sets it down on the mantle and walks over to his son. "Come with me, young man," Daddy says seriously. Mickey takes his father's hand, turning around for comfort from Momma and Roddy, but their still faces only prophecy the worst.

Once in the master bedroom, Jack picks his son up and seats him on the end of the big bed, then squats down in front of him. Mickey knows this is a showdown like in *Hopalong Cassidy*. "Little boys don't play with dolls," Daddy slowly, emphatically begins, pronouncing "dolls" more like "dalls." "Only sissies play with dalls and no son of mine is going to be a sissy. Your mother is going to give all those dalls back. Do you understand?"

Mickey is in shock. He doesn't understand, but it clearly doesn't matter. Daddy picks him up off the bed and walks the dazed boy back into the living room. Mickey wipes a tear angrily from his cheek and breaks lose from his father, running off to his bedroom. Mother gets up to console him.

"Jean, goddammit, leave him be," Daddy insists.

Mother stares off down the hall after her son, whose muffled sobs fill the house. "It's Christmas. We should be a happy family." Mother begins to cry and she goes to Mickey.

"Jean, come back here," Daddy demands.

"Drink your eggnog, Jack. I'll only be a minute." She disappears down the hall into the youngster's room.

"It's the dolls, isn't it, Dad?" Rodney asks.

"Not anymore, it isn't, son," Daddy growls, sipping his eggnog.

To tell your story
you have to be
willing to change
your story.

SHIRLEY COHEN

HOW WILL I KNOW?

How will I know? What does it feel like when plaque strangles a brain? Is it painful or would I have no idea it's happening?

Should fate and statistics decree that I become one of the many Alzheimer's afflicted, will I know what happened to my consciousness when I slip into Alzheimer's from lucidity or dementia or life as I knew it? How can I even know when I have wandered into dementia from ordinary age-related forgetfulness? Or whether and when dementia has progressed further into Alzheimer's? Does anyone know? Has anyone been able to travel between lucidity and the twilight zone to tell us what it feels like when you slip over the edge?

Normal age-related memory loss is here and now for me. In the early stages of dementia or, if anyone can be certain, Alzheimer's, there are apparently moments of clarity while one is between life and another planet. In those moments of clarity, is it possible that one is aware of how it felt when you were in the other dimension? And when do those moments in one's life stop coming back?

Might I find my true love in Harry's Haven or an Alzheimer's-type care facility? A lot of people seem to attach to a fellow patient and blissfully forget they might have been or still are married to someone else or that anyone else exists. It's like they begin a new self and maybe a new adventure. That could be wonderful while it lasts, for the patients. Not so much for the patient's loved ones who are still here on this planet!

Alzheimer's victims and even the dementia-afflicted say and do really funny and outrageous things. It's not funny, but it is. There has to be some humor for the loved ones left behind.

Can it be that in that Alzheimer's dimension, I might also forget my conditional terms for loving and just love? Can it be that I might forget to be critical, judgmental and forget about trying to control the other and my own life and just be in it? It might be a wonderful and joyful life until it slowly kills me. And then there's nothing funny about it. How will I know?

I wonder how it feels. Hopefully when I'm out of my mind, I won't feel the pain of shutting down, walking away from my body, and leaving my mind behind. And where is it that I would go? Have I any awareness of that place? Or is it just a slow fade to black?

Is there terrible pain or how much awareness and or feeling would I have in the process? Does anyone know?

I have a taste of what it feels like to be in the aura of a migraine headache. I've had these headaches since childhood. In fact since the second grade when my mother was called to come get me from school. Could I have had the stress in the second grade that medicine can only guess brings on a migraine headache? The extreme pain has diminished over the years, but the brain fart lingers. The last migraine headache I had very recently, as usual began as an ocular migraine, or migraine with aura. I see flashing or shimmering lights, zigzagging lines, or stars, or psychedelic images. It usually starts with blind spots in my field of vision. It feels like I'm having a transient ischemic accident which is probably a mini stroke and we all seem to accumulate those. Some happen all the time often without ever knowing we've had them.

During this relatively brief time in the aura of a migraine, I remember once sitting at the computer and feeling totally alien to the keys and buttons. I had no idea what to do with them. If and while I'm attempting to have a conversation, I can't remember a single name that I know very well or connect the name with a person. It is a brief interlude and frustrating while it's happening, but having experienced it before I know I will regain my memory . . . at least to my normal age-related forgetfulness.

What's frightening to me is being aware of losing absolute control of my mind. I am aware of what partial control feels like. But that feeling that I'm a stranger to myself and everything else . . . is that what Alzheimer's feels like or would I even be aware that I've gone into outer space? And then maybe total forgetfulness could be a blessing in light of what's to come.

This is not by any stretch a joyful subject and maybe not a useful one—either to me or to anyone listening. But I can't help wondering!

INSECURITY & GRAVITY

One of Peter's abbreviated and profound notes on memoir writing: "Writing about the darkest times in my life, I can now see that my insecurities were almost always the root of my suffering . . ."

Such a plaintive truth . . . so familiar to me from as far back as I can remember. I don't know when my own insecurities developed. Probably as I grappled with the rules of how I am required to be in the world. Maybe insecurities are hereditary. Maybe they are accumulated like barnacles on a whale as we learn how we must fit into society. How to look, how to think, how to behave to be an accepted member. I think insecurity might be the root of all evil, money only second in the world . . .

It has been said that only exceptional minds can recall childhood before age six. I recall little if any of my childhood stress before multiplication tables came or didn't come into my life. I don't even remember what age that was. I do remember my father tried all sorts of tricks and finally attempted to bully me into memorizing those tables. It was then I realized insecurity or maybe more inadequacy, in ever conquering math at least.

I had no truly dark times in my life. Compared to real darkness, I led a charmed, even dull life. Growing up in the fifties was an idyllic time just after the great wars end when America was at her finest. We happily collected papers for paper drives at school. We sang patriotic songs and America was proud of herself. I wasn't aware of any true insecurity other than the self-inflicted kind suffered in adolescence when I was certain I did not fit in.

Adolescence I do recall, vividly. I wanted to be invisible all through puberty. As inconspicuous as I could be, convinced I was the only one with adolescent acne and a developing body that didn't measure up to the other girls.

There was, though, becoming aware of being a Semite at a very young age at the end of the Great War when anti-Semitism raged. I'm certain it had a powerful affect on the collective Jewish psyche. Even as a second-generation, American-born Jew to a practically secular Jewish family, with little background or understanding of Jews or Jewish history, I felt the magnitude of the Holocaust. I felt it in my bones and childishly feared for my life. Even though I lived in the U. S. of A. and a pogrom wasn't conceivable here, still I believed that it was bound to come. That might have put a little dent in my childhood security! Even now, given our current political climate, with neo-Nazis on the march, I still, in my worst nightmares, imagine that it could happen here!

Insecurity may be a way of life! A little heavy to lug around. Maybe designed to keep us humble or in some cases, the other extreme, to overcompensate in the opposite direction. In any case, always self-defeating. I have no doubt that "insecurities are almost always the root of my suffering" although to what degree I suffer is arguable.

Can I overcome insecurity at this late date? I still slouch. I try hard to straighten up (pun intended), but I am now in the end, defying gravity, the gravity of the universe and the gravity of my own resistance to change.

The mighty force of physical gravity and age pull me down. Try as I might, there is no defying the gravity of the universe. It sometimes pulls me down into the doldrums. It pulls words and memories out of my reach. My head feels too heavy to hold up. It bows toward my feet. My shoulders hunch. My body slowly moves to return to the fetal position.

In the sunset of my life, rising above where I've been, is daunting. I have till now, been unsuccessful in creating meaningful change. My resistance to change is strong and change is scary.

Maybe insecurity is not so terrible. Maybe there are worse things. Revisiting chickenpox might be worse. Shingles is definitely worse. Humor might be the antidote to insecurity . . . and snake bite!!

THE SEA

I have no recollection of the story my mother tells when as a baby, my father dropped me into the Atlantic Ocean! As the story goes, it was on a fine summer day at a family outing on the beach at Far Rockaway, Long Island, New York. My father had taken me out into the reasonably gentle waves and apparently the two of us were enjoying some play time in the water when a rogue wave swept me out of his arms and under the water.

The sea coughed me up and Dad fished me out but from my first swallow of sea water, the sea became an irresistible, magnetic force that drew me in. La Mer instilled in me a little fear and a lot of healthy respect and total fascination for the oceans that cover so much of our blue planet, which now are rising to inundate low-lying land first and upward as we carelessly warm the globe. Rachel Carson said last century: "Only within the moment of time represented by the present century has one species—man—acquired significant power to alter the nature of the world."

And that was last century . . . In the meantime, I'm very fortunate to have spent as much of my life as I could possibly manage in and near the sea. The sea had allowed me to revel in it. It has thrilled and tumbled and pummeled and knocked me about but always I had run back for more.

As a kid in the good old days, when so much more of our innocence was intact, my friends and I used to take the big red car (Pacific Electric train) for a nickel—or sometimes hitchhike from L.A. to the beach and spend the whole of every weekend in the water, coming out only for a hamburger and running back in.

Years later, I never longed for the sea so much as when I was on a location in Tucson, Arizona. No matter the season, it was so hot and dry everyone spoke through lips that were painfully cracked. I felt like I was drowning in the sands of the desert. All I could think about was how far away the sea was. I dreamed of cool breezes on Hawaiian islands.

Through the years I've spent countless hours of the most pleasurable time at tide pools watching the inhabitants go about their business in microscopic oceans and combed beaches from Santa Monica to New Zealand looking to discover a treasure: an ancient coin, a piece of sea glass, a sea-sculpted piece of driftwood, stone or shell, the thrill of finding something that the seas might bring on the tides from faraway places and sunken ships.

I thought one day I might even find a note in a bottle from someone from some place in time who might have been stranded on a deserted island or who was desperately seeking to communicate with someone or anyone in another world or maybe someone just looking for a date—the note in the bottle perhaps being the precursor to match.com!

All along and maybe since that first swallow of sea water, I have been awestruck by what they used to call tidal waves but now known to be tsunami. I read a book in the sixties written by a stewardess who was there when a thirty-five- to fifty-foot wave engulfed Hilo, Hawaii. Just reading the book I was mesmerized and terrified all at once.

I used to have a recurring dream of fifty-foot waves coming to some unfamiliar beach, and while quaking and scared out of my mind, I miraculously walked through the wave to the other side as I had dived through or ducked under much less formidable waves many times in reality.

I also dreamed often that I could breathe underwater, seventy years before I saw Aquaman do it. I interpreted those dreams to mean that I would survive, if not enjoy the oceans' worst moods, but in reality, when I was in my twenties, my confidence and conceit were dashed during my final reckoning with the sea.

It came when I was lured into the water at a small cove at Little Corona del Mar where I was enjoying a beach day with friends. Red danger flags flew, warning of dangerous rip currents. Despite them, a couple of the young men who actually had lifeguard training were in the water, one along with his kids. The water was strangely still and they said, "C'mon in . . . look how calm and beautiful it is," and I couldn't resist. In no time at all, there came a series of powerful waves that sucked everything, including the shore, out to meet the next breaking wave without time to catch a breath in between huge breaking waves.

After managing to push through the break of just a few of those monsters, I became exhausted and, while hyperventilating, literally saw my life flash before my eyes. I screamed to my friend Perry, the lifeguard for help! He grabbed me around the neck and we paddled furiously as a wave caught and carried us to the shore, a killer wave that pounded us onto the beach, beat us up like we had been in a giant tumbling washing machine. I lay there on the beach gasping for air and feeling as though my lungs were collapsed.

I could never bring myself to swim in the ocean again. No more the fool who rushed in where angels fear to tread . . . water. Sad for lost innocence, humbled by the sea's anger, and sadder yet for what had become of the ocean in the short time while I grew up. Heartsick about the pollution that poisoned sea creatures and the plastic waste that choked them to death . . .

But I still love to sit on a beach or watch from the end of a pier, those waves in all their moods and colors and enjoy watching intrepid surfers trick those waves from wiping them out.

I now reside in a retirement home for showfolk and disillusioned mermaids. I am far from the dumb kid who ran blithely into the ocean's open arms. She had finally taught me true humility when she smacked me down for the last time.

I flop around now in our little pool and try to imagine the smell of chlorine is the salty sea air. I can't do the butterfly stroke anymore, let alone the dolphin kick, mermaids' and dolphins' and manatees' mode of locomotion. Somebody suggested that sailors and pirates who had been at sea for far too long, having consumed a lot of grog may have sighted some attractive manatees and invented mermaids! I really miss the sea!

Last week, our great activities department treated us to a wonderful day at Ventura Harbor. It couldn't have been a more perfect day.

We were let loose and left to our own devices but advised not to cross the road that separates the harbor village from the beach and sea. But the siren call of the ocean drew me to it and I snuck across the street. I climbed the little dune at the shore and thrilled to the salt air breeze. The sea was restless with whitecaps on the dark water. Signs warned of rip currents and danger. Still there were surfers braving the small but mighty waves. I didn't have time to stay long but, always scanning the sand, I found a little piece of driftwood that looked for all the world like the little dog that I am forever hankering after!

Shirley Cohen

BRETT HADLEY

There is much I miss as I reach the sunset of my life, but near the top of my list is "Taps." That long and mournful call to reflect on the events of the day's struggles, to put them into perspective and put the day to rest.

I don't know when "Taps" was first blown over the camps of war, but I can picture it in a time before long-range impersonal warfare; a time before gunpowder and the longbow, when combat was hand-to-hand and face-to-face with the man who was there to kill you and you, him. A time when war had rules and a certain degree of civility, as if that concept could ever be applied to wholesale killing. A time when "Retreat" was blown at sundown, and each army withdrew to their own camps to retrieve their wounded and bury their dead, to rest for tomorrow's fight and to reevaluate the day. In my mind, I can hear that lonesome call—and to know it had been a good day, you had fought well and had survived; you had killed but you had survived to fight again tomorrow. But for what? Put that aside for a saner time, your job is to survive tomorrow; albeit for the glory of someone else.

Our current struggles may or may not be as grave, but still it is good to reflect on your day; did it have anything of value for you or someone else, was it a productive day? Will tomorrow have merit?

I would love to hear "Taps" blow over the campus to put the day to rest and to sleep.

Petar Sardelich

PETAR SARDELICH

AMERICANIZATION OF A MAN FROM DALMATIA

As a child I always dreamed of faraway places and strange worlds. Most of these dreams became a reality on the first of August 1961, when at 9:00 a.m. aboard the *Queen Mary*, I arrived in New York harbor. The first thing I saw on the starboard side was the magnificent skyline of New York, and on the portside the Statue of Liberty, the world's most recognizable symbol of freedom.

At that moment I felt as if I had awoken from a dream and found myself in the magical town and country of my dreams.

Once I came here, I was completely overcome with worries about my immediate future. I had many questions about what was in front of me. Will there be anyone waiting for me? What will I do if there was no one there I know? So many worries about my future. I've always been insecure, as a human being from a small country, a small town, not knowing the language, the people, the customs and everything else that is there for a man finding himself alone in a foreign land.

I am sure that this kind of feeling overcomes every new arrival to this magical land.

Most Americans, when they hear me talk, ask where my accent is from. I tell them that I am Dalmatian, which always shocks them as they know very little about Dalmatia, or where it is. The only thing they know about the name is a "Dalmatian dog," one of the most popular dog breeds in US, a symbol for American firefighters, often found in most firefighting stations in the country. That is why, when I say that I am a Dalmatian, I am often asked in jest: "Where are your black dots?" For that reason, I must explain that Dalmatia is a coastal region of Croatia, and that Dalmatian dogs come from that part of the world.

Croatia is one of the countries that broke away from the Communist Yugoslavia during the Balkan war of 1991. After ten centuries of being overrun by foreign forces, my old country became independent again.

Having lived most of my life here in US, it makes me that much more confused about my true feelings inside my soul, whether my real home is Croatia or the United States. I too often felt a "Stranger in a Strange World," a feeling which became my constant companion, an exile at the crossroads of my life without an anchor to keep me steady. Not only here in the USA, but also the town of my childhood, the country of my birth, with the people I love, and finally inside of my own soul.

My life here has been a constant sorrow for leaving my parents, my brothers, my friends, my girlfriend, my old childhood home, my Island of Korcula, and my old country Croatia.

What helped to keep steady my soul, and my feelings about becoming American, has been love for my son (who was born American), my Croatian and American families, the "Old Country" and the ability to go back twenty-three times since I left.

By nature, I am a wanderer. Since I came to US, I have had twenty-three different addresses, and thirteen different full-time jobs.

Before I came to US, my first job in Croatia was working as an electrotechician and a light opera singer. My first job here in the US was working in a San Pedro car wash, washing cars for two weeks. I left that job in order to be able to attend school at the Americanization Center.

I got a night job at a local bakery. This was the only job I was ever fired from. The second night there, I was assigned to take baked loaves of bread from the oven and stack them onto a large rack. Pulling the bread out of the hot oven, the loafs were so hot, that, after handling about a dozen of them, despite my wearing double canvas gloves, my fingers felt like they were on fire, making me to drop two loaves on the ground. As the foreman was in the same area, when he saw me dropping the bread on the ground, he immediately fired me.

In the meantime I met two young Dalmatian immigrants in San Pedro who played accordions, and one of them had a good singing voice. We formed a Dalmatian trio and played dance music and sang our folk songs, Italian and Latin, as well as some Russian and Hebrew songs and dances. We were so popular in Southern California Croatian and other Slavic halls and churches, that we became the standard group playing for most weddings, birthdays, and similar celebrations from Bixby, Arizona, to San Diego, and all of the Los Angeles area as well.

The additional earnings helped a lot for my ability to pay the college tuition. As luck would have it, with StarKist tuna cannery being owned by a Dalmatian-born owner, I got a full-time job working there. My first job was as a night-time janitor cleaning the plant after the daily crew prepared tuna fish for canning. Next, I was moved to the warehouse where we packed the finished product for distribution. My final job there I worked in combined areas of mail room and the Cannery's records storage.

At night I attended the Columbia College for TV, Film and M.P. This, along with the full-time job at the cannery and playing with the Dalmatian Trio, I averaged some eighty-five hours of work per week.

Approximately five years after coming to American shores, and before my graduation from Columbia College, I got a job in the NBC mail room. My job at NBC lasted close to thirty-one years, where I worked in a variety of jobs.

After year and a half at NBC, I interviewed for the job of KNBC production coordinator. There were thirteen applicants interviewing for the job. Some of them had worked for the company much longer that I did. Most of them already had college degrees, while I was still in college, yet despite my heavy accent, talking English like I just came off the boat, I got that job!

Getting the production job at KNBC, no one was more surprised that I was. The first day on the job, I was sitting in my new office with no one there except two secretaries who also knew nothing about the job. The reason being, that day was June 6, 1968. The day Robert Kennedy was assassinated in a Los Angeles hotel. All production management was at the hotel and/or the hospital running the TV coverage of the assassination. So what do I do? I read all the papers available in the office to look like I knew what I was doing.

Almost a year after that day and almost exactly three years of being employed by NBC, I was promoted to KNBC production manager.

My NBC career defies rhyme and reason. My success there, some seven years after *Queen Mary* brought me into the USA, without any knowledge of the English language, I was able to work at the largest TV station in the USA.

I am so grateful to America for giving me the chance for a better life. Even more, my heartfelt feelings and thanks go to all my American coworkers, and numerous American friends, who accepted me as a member of their global families. Additionally, I am thankful for the American way of life. Having lived here for over fifty-seven years, I must admit that I am much more an American than a Croat.

By achieving one of my biggest dreams of integrating myself as a productive America citizen, my Americanization became complete.

We do not let our
experiences define
us. We use them as
we would a looking
glass, to view the
world anew.

DAVID KRAMER

THE BORROWED SUIT

When you think about it, youth is like a borrowed suit.

We enter this world bald, toothless, wrinkled and with no control over our bowels. Though it may seem to take forever, in just a relative few years, we grow into our suits (Disguises) and we appear vital and attractive. Forget what's underneath. For both sexes, the suit begins to fit.

After the awkward years pass, we've grown vital and attractive. Now slim of waistline, straight of back, we smile with gleaming teeth. Men's backs are muscular, women's breasts begin interesting the opposite sex.

The borrowed suit lasts through our educations, remains as we seek life partners, the hunt made easier with thick, dark hair and the assurance of youth. Mercifully, we have no hint or memory of what's beneath the shiny exterior and go about our lives clueless . . . until the varnish begins to crack. At first, we think it's a fault in the mirror, but soon enough we realize a change is taking place.

Luckily, the transition isn't immediate. Competitive men and women fight it every step of the way.

We pack gyms and fitness classes. Men stop seeing barbers and start going to stylists who secretly cover the gray with dye. At first going to a women's hair salon was a bit uncomfortable, but the girls understood what drove the men, and there was very little snickering. The women were fighting their own battles with concealing stretch marks and considering surgery on breasts at least, and for some a whole new, younger face.

Meanwhile, the real us has begun to stir. As though waking from a forty- to fifty-year nap, stretching, yawning, scratching, looking about for themselves, an exercise made tougher by face-lifts and diets, hair dye and hairpieces . . . but slowly, with a certain gentility, our real selves take what is theirs.

Men's muscles are replaced by drooping guy breasts, their hirsute adornment by a pate of gleaming shiny skins, with parentheses of white hair, like an atoll surrounding a calm lagoon. Their genitals have lost some importance and become hidden beneath a well-earned beer belly. Visits increase to dentists and physicians. We're self-conscious, worrying at first the effect has on the opposite sex.

But women hardly notice. They're busily fighting their own battles, above and below, the thickening waistline.

Eventually, and by the grace of whatever gods may be, we grow less concerned with the changes, and relax, and like the Lone Ranger, we return to yesteryear, relatively unconcerned.

THE END . . . ? ? ?

CONTRIBUTORS

RICHARD "DUKE" ANDERSON was raised in North Hollywood. He served in the US Navy as a radio operator during World War II in the Pacific theater. Later, he spent over thirty years working in radio, television, and movies, while raising his children Paul, Karen, Stacey, and Duke. He became a resident of MPTF in May 2013.

WILLIAM BLINN was born in Toledo, Ohio. Bill attended the American Academy of Dramatic Arts. A prolific writer and producer, he created the series: *FAME, Our House, Starsky & Hutch, The New Land,* and *The Lazarus Syndrome,* among others. As well, Bill wrote many TV movies and mini-series including *Shane, A Man Called Intrepid, Brian's Song,* and the history-making *Roots.*

HENRI BOLLINGER: As a teenager in London, Henri wanted to be an actor. He appeared in the role of Alain in *Johnny Frenchman* in 1945, *Great Expectations* in 1946, and toured England in Lillian Hellman's *Watch On the Rhine* in 1946. He emigrated to the United States in 1947. Not able to further his goal as an actor, he turned to publicity. He was known for his creative and effective publicity and promotion campaigns. Henri held key positions with numerous entertainment industry, community, and service organizations. He served five terms as President of the Publicists Guild of America and chaired the Publicists Guild award luncheon for fifty years. President and founding member of the Entertainment Publicists Professional Society (EPPS), he also served on the Foreign Film Committee of the Academy of Motion Picture Arts & Sciences, chaired the Communications Committee of the Hollywood Entertainment Museum, served on the public relations committee of the Academy of Television Arts & Sciences, chaired the publications and publicity committee of the International Cinematographers Society, and was instrumental in forming a publicity and marketing class at UCLA extension. A Henri Bollinger Memorial scholarship fund was established to provide funds to individuals with a passion for public relations to study a certificate in Strategic Branding and Public Relations at UCLA Extension. Henri moved to MPTF in February 2018 after undergoing two brain surgeries. While there, he enjoyed participating in the Grey Quill Society, Tai Chi, working out at the gym, taking art and ukulele lessons, and playing poker. Henri passed away just six months after moving into MPTF, but all these activities brought him much joy and gave him a sense of purpose, which made those six months at MPTF memorable.

 SANDY BOLLINGER moved to California when she was eleven years old, however her accent leaves no doubt that she was Brooklyn-born. She met her husband, Henri, at work when she was eighteen, married him at twenty-one, and during their fifty-four years together, they raised three children and were blessed with four grandchildren. She worked side-by-side with Henri in his public relations firm. Upon entering MPTF, Sandy was elected to the residents' council on which she still serves. In addition to working out in the gym and pool, she is currently active with the Grey Quill Society and Channel 22. She is surprised and delighted to find herself an emerging writer and performer.

 SHIRLEY COHEN in her early years typed scripts for some of the great writers, beginning on *Playhouse 90*. Experiencing those words flow on the page seemed like it must be easy to write them, but she tried it and found that it certainly is not as easy as it looks. Not at all. Still, she enjoyed a world of inspiration being surrounded by those magical words in various stages of production behind the scenes for fifty years. Most rewarding was being producer Walter Seltzer's assistant on some major films. To name a few: *Soylent Green, The Omega Man,* and *Will Penny.*

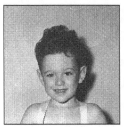 MICKEY COTTRELL was immediately captivated by the movies when his first such experience, *Song of the South*, sent him dancing out of the theater singing "Zip-A-Dee-Do-Dah." A year later, he became a victim of the Polio epidemic and Mickey lived with other youngsters for a year in the Polio Center of Charity Hospital in New Orleans, four hours from his home in

northern Louisiana. Most weekends his family visited. Cottrell is currently completing a memoir novella, *The Firemen's Equipment* about his time there.

After his family moved to Little Rock and winning his high school's annual talent shows for four consecutive years (singing songs from *Oklahoma*, *West Side Story*, *My Fair Lady*, and *Camelot*) Mickey won the University of Arkansas's Freshmen/Sophomore and Junior/Senior Best Performances. At the Arkansas Art Center, Cottrell excelled onstage in several well-reviewed performances, including "Mitch" in *A Streetcar Named Desire* and "Marat" in *Marat/Sade*.

Mickey spent two seasons (1968–1969) at the Guthrie Theater in Minneapolis where he played the lead in Sam Shepard's *Red Cross*, and made his Broadway debut in the Sir Tyrone Guthrie directed *House of Atreus* in 1968. From 1970–1972, he traveled throughout Western Europe, settling in London and choosing the Ashram life before returning to the States. In 1980, he moved to Los Angeles, programming and operating a revival cinema, the Loyola Movie Palace and then becoming the national PR director and LA programmer for Landmark Theatres. From 1985–1988, Cottrell headed up the entertainment department of Josh Baran & Associates, overseeing the victorious Academy Awards campaigns for Best Docs, *Artie Shaw: Time is All You Got* (1986) and *Broken Rainbow* (1987). In 1988, Cottrell oversaw PR for Wim Wenders' *Wings of Desire*, the first foreign language film to exceed a million dollars at the US box office.

As an actor, Mickey has appeared in over fifty films, TV shows, and plays, including *My Own Private Idaho*, *Star Trek: The Next Generation* and *Little Murders*. As a publicist, Mickey has repped over two hundred films or respective artists.

 **MIMI COZZENS:** Affectionately called Mimi before she was a year old, both she and sister Dorothy Faith were child models for the John Robert Powers Agency in New York City (Mimi booked her first job at age three and a half).

She made her Broadway debut in Neil Simon's *I Ought to Be in Pictures* when she went on for Joyce Van Patten. Her national tours include *The Prisoner of Second Avenue*, *Mornings at Seven*, and *Same Time, Next Year*, as well as the original LA/Denver tour of *Tribute* starring Jack Lemmon.

Mimi has divided her time between film and TV work. As to the former she has appeared in *The Master*, *Spring Break*, *Night of the Cyclone*, *Live Wire*, *The Pandora Project*, *Dandelion Dharma*, *What Would Jesus Do?*, *Christmas Mail*, and the soon to be released *The Last Tour*. On the smaller screen, Mimi had guest/co-star roles on such sitcoms as *The Mindy Project, The Jeffersons, Seinfeld, 3rd Rock from the Sun, Malcolm in the Middle, The Golden Girls, Will & Grace, Greek, One Big Family* starring Danny Thomas, and *Carol & Company* starring Carol Burnett. Dramatic series work include *Cold Case, Providence, Chicago Hope, The Practice, Knot's Landing, Columbo, St.Elsewhere, Star Trek,* and *Numb3rs.*

Commercially, Mimi has pitched everything from detergents and fabric softeners to cough syrups and headache medicines.

A member of the LA and national boards of SAG-AFTRA, and involved in the historic vote to merge the two, she also serves on the executive committee of the Performers Peer Group of the Academy of TV Arts & Sciences.

JOHN DEL REGNO began his acting career doing theater in New York, where he worked at the New York Shakespeare Public Theater. Hollywood beckoned and he moved there and acted in over fifty top-of-the-show guest spots on TV plus several films which can be seen nowadays at 2 a.m. on HBO. His greatest achievement is raising his daughter Claire to adulthood.

RAYMOND DE TOURNAY is a Los Angeles–based writer with a career as a producer/director/editor in television broadcasting and his own video production company. His client list included major corporations plus the Reagan Presidential Library and The Carter Center in Atlanta. He studied novel writing at UCLA and is a member of the Director's Guild of America. Recent print credits include non-fiction articles published in *Road & Track*, the *Los Angeles Times* and the *Los Angeles Daily News*. He is now retired from television production and living in the Los Angeles area where he continues to write.

ANNE FAULKNER: A true late bloomer. In Ohio: Metromedia executive in TV division, an actor and director in local theater wherever she lived. Mid-life: off to New York and Los Angeles becoming a full-time actor. Today: writer, actor, and mother of two, grandmother to seven, great-grandmother to eleven children, and now in 2019 an amazing four great-great-grandchildren!

ALFRED BRETT HADLEY is an actor who has performed in several movies, lots of TV shows, including eighteen years on *The Young and the Restless*, many TV commercials, and a great deal of live theater. Today he is focusing on writing life stories and finishing his novel.

LISABETH HUSH. New York City born and bred. Couldn't wait to get away. Had her SAG card and first job a few weeks after coming to LA. Became a for-life member of The Actors Studio, then Theatre West. Loves stage work, film, and TV. Poetry just started pouring from her in the '70s. Oh, yes, the more she learns of her family, she believes she's fulfilled all their hidden desires to act. Lucky Lisabeth.

DAVID KRAMER: After discharge from the United States Navy David was faced with the necessity of doing something other than attending classes and saluting. He chose film stardom. After bartending, cab driving and free-lancing his meager art skills for five years, and doing very, very little acting, he saw the writing on the wall. It said, "Press Release: Do entertainment publicity. It looked like fun and you get to dress swell and act import-ant." I thought he could do that, and did for nearly fifty years, met a lot of nifty people, married twice, and sired two great kids.

ANTHONY LAWRENCE was a prolific TV writer who also co-wrote three Elvis Presley films, then wrote and produced a three-hour Presley biopic. Tony has received four WGA nominations and is on the Writers' Guild list of 101 best-written TV series for *Gunsmoke*, *Columbo*, and *The Fugitive*.

MAGGIE MALOOLY was born in Chicago, Illinois. Relocating to Los Angeles, she has appeared in more than three hundred TV commercials, twenty-six roles on various TV series, and hosted morning talk shows. Maggie has produced, written, and hosted TV and radio travel segments, and produced three live appearances of Rock Hudson in Argentina and Brazil. Her most cherished and treasured production: four children and four grandchildren.

DEBORAH ROGOSIN was born and raised in California. She lived around the corner from her future husband, Joel Rogosin, and started dating him when she was eighteen. After two years of college, she married Joel and dropped out of school in order to support him during his last year at Stanford. They moved to LA after college and started a family—three daughters in five years—while Joel broke into showbiz. Deborah returned to her studies, pursuing a masters degree in art when she developed retinitis pigmentosa, a genetic condition that led to her gradual loss of sight. Undeterred, she pursued a degree in psychology and has been a licensed psychotherapist for thirty-six years.

JOEL ROGOSIN is a veteran Hollywood "hyphenate"—a writer/producer/director—with over thirty years of experience in the entertainment industry, and perhaps hundreds of credits on primetime TV series and movies. On two occasions he also produced *The Jerry Lewis Labor Day Telethon*, twenty-one live hours, for the Muscular Dystrophy Association. He has written screenplays, poetry, two produced stage musicals, and a published memoir, *Writing a Life*, and conducts innovative writing workshops, The Creative Adventure, in various nationwide venues. He and his wife, Deborah, a marriage and family therapist, have three daughters and five grandchildren and are looking forward to their first great-grandson.

PETER SARDELICH was born in Croatia where he lived twenty-seven years before coming to the US. In Croatia, his main job was as a singer in a light opera chorus. After arriving in the US, he attended Columbia College of Hollywood where he got a BA in telecommunications. After graduation, his career in TV lasted over thirty-two years: NBC LA, twenty-nine years, NBC International in Hong Kong, two and a half years. One year as an adviser to the President of HRT, Croatian Radio/TV network in Zagreb, Croatia, and one year for Hallmark Channel in Denver, Colorado. After college graduation, he taught a variety of TV subjects: at Columbia College, six years, LACC, six years, and Pasadena City College, five and a half years. He retired on the last calendar day of the twentieth century.

ALAN SLOAN began his career in the industry in the mailroom at ABC in 1954. He worked at Ted Bates advertising as a media buyer and then as a salesman at CBS. In 1963, under their auspices, he took mid-career break earning a Ph.D. in political behavior at M.I.T., doing his field work in Peru. Upon returning to CBS, he eventually became VP, General Manager of WCBS-TV. In 1970, with his wife and three children, he left NY for Hollywood where he worked as a company executive as well as an independent producer-writer on numerous television movies and series. He retired to Florida in 1999 where he became active in senior issues. He returned to California in 2013 and has served on the Executive Council of AARP California for the past six years.

MADI SMITH-LAWRENCE was a concert violinist and dancer, although not at the same time. She has worked in the entertainment business for over forty-five years. She received her AF of M, AFTRA, and SAG cards in 1954 when she was put under contract to Paramount. She worked at NBC for ten years as a scheduler in broadcast operations and control, and as liaison between NBC and the Directors Guild of America. Following her years at NBC, Madi worked as an executive assistant for the Smothers Brothers, Bobby Darin, Danny Arnold, and Norman Lear, among others.

JOAN TANNEN was born in White Plains, New York. She has been a resident at the MPTF for close to twelve years. She was a secretary at Screen Gems, the Directors Guild of America, and CBS. Joan's husband, Charles, was an actor under contract to 20th Century Fox and continued acting until 1963 when he became a television comedy writer. In addition to her writing, Joan enjoys oil painting, Wii golf, and bowling, and improv, and writes and produces for Chanel 22 and the *Resident Gazette*.

JOHN TOWEY: Broadway, Off-Broadway, regional theatre, film and TV veteran, John, a professional actor for the past fifty years (AEA, SAG-AFTRA), has portrayed over one hundred characters on stages across the country. He acted for three consecutive seasons each at: Arena Stage in Washington, DC, The Guthrie Theatre in Minneapolis, and The Public Theatre in New York. Since moving to L.A. from New York in 1990, John has guest-starred in over forty television shows: *Murphy Brown, The X-Files, Empty Nest, Fresh Prince of Bel Air*, and *Crossing Jordan*, to name a few. He holds a BFA degree from The Goodman School of Drama in Chicago. Originally trained as a pianist, some of his music may be heard on his website: www.john-towey.com.

KAY WEISSMAN: My birth certificate says Wilma Kay Friedman, born 1936, Detroit, Michigan. I changed my name to Antonia Flores when I became a Spanish dancer and performed with Jose Greco throughout Europe at seventeen. Then I got my SAG card as Kay Freeman in 1973, to be a bridesmaid in *The Godfather*. There were many names and performances in between, studying with Uta Hagen, Herbert Berghoff, Charles Nelson Reilly, Warren Robertson, and every actor and director I ever worked with. My greatest joy came in 1996 when I married Murray Weissman, P.R. executive and became, Mrs. Murray Weissman!!!

GRATITUDE

This book would not be possible without the tireless efforts of so many generous people who donated their precious time. Deepest gratitude and recognition to:

Karen Richardson, for literally putting this book together, working around the clock to make it happen, and being a general rock star.

Bob Beitcher, for supporting the Quills at every juncture and taking time out of his very busy schedule to assist in so many ways. MPTF is the most incredible place, and we are so grateful to have him at the helm.

Patricia Santana for generously donating her time, and talent to create the beautiful artwork that graces our cover.

Ed Stauss for the often overlooked but vital job of proofreading.

Rachel Berman for spending countless hours cataloging the incredible library of poetry from Lisbeth Hush, and always supporting the work of the Quills.

Ben Cowitt for being a wonderful supporter.

Jen Clymer and the entire Channel 22 team for helping the Grey Quills at every opportunity.

The MPTF staff who go above and beyond to take care of our residents, and ensure we have coffee and treats every Thursday morning.

Peter Dunne for everything, and for contributing his artistic talents to the book as well. Peter would start each Grey Quill meeting off by writing an insightful thought or quote he'd come up with on the whiteboard. Some of these are sprinkled throughout the book, with his charming drawing accompanying them.

All the Quills, past and present: Thank you. I am honored to know you and grateful for you all. We remember the Quills we have lost and honor them by including some of their pieces in this book. Richard 'Duke' Anderson, Henri Bollinger, David Kramer, and Joel Rogosin, and we miss you, especially on Thursdays.

And to you, dear reader, for buying this book and supporting our group.

We all thank you for that!

—Ed.

Made in the USA
San Bernardino, CA
23 June 2020